COMPILED BY THE EDITORS OF HIPPOCRENE BOOKS

HIPPOCRENE BOOKS, INC.
New York

ISBN 0-7818-0752-2

For information, address:
HIPPOCRENE BOOKS, INC.
171 Madison Avenue
New York, NY 10016

Printed in the United States of America.

African Region Love Poems

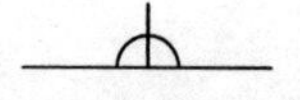

ANCIENT EGYPTIAN (Egypt)

The sickness of love

I will go home and lay me down
I will make as if I am ill
My neighbours will come to visit me
And my beloved will be there with them
Then there will be no need of physicians
Since it is she who knows what truly ails me.

I am yours

I am yours,
So where will your heart now turn?

Would you turn away
If you seek to be fed?
If you long to caress
My thighs and my breasts,
Be a glutton for me.

Would you turn away
If you need to be clothed?
Surely I am clothes enough.

Would you turn away
If you hunger?
Take my breasts,
Abundant is what they offer.

O happy is the day of your sweet embrace!

The trap

The goose cries out
Snared by my bait —
Your love snares me
And I know no means of escape.
Now I shall take up my nets
Not knowing what to tell my mother,
Since to her each day I return
When I am loaded down with catch.
But today I did not set my trap —
Today your love trapped me.

Unique is a maiden

Here begin the Words of the Great Dispenser of Entertainment . . .

Unique is a maiden, without peer
Comelier than all mankind.

Behold, she is like the Star Goddess rising
At the beginning of an auspicious year.

She is of sheen surpassing, radiant of skin
Lovely of eyes with which to gaze.

Sweet are her lips with which to speak —
She has not a word too much.

Long of neck, bright of nipples
True sapphire is her hair
Her arms surpass gold
Her fingers are like lotus flowers.

Curving buttocks, slim-waisted
Her thighs extend her perfection
Fair of gait as she treads upon the earth.

She has seized my heart with her embrace
She makes the necks of all men
Turn away dazzled at the very sight of her.

Joyous is he who embraces her
He is like the chief of all lovers.

Her going forth is seen
Just as she is — a unique maiden.

BEMBA (Zambia)

You who spurn me

You who spurn me, today you've returned
You who spurn me, today you've returned
Why have you returned?
You who spurn me, today you've returned
What will you offer me now, poor soul that I am?
What will you offer me now, poor soul that I am?
What will you offer me now, what now, poor soul that you are?

BERBER (Morocco, Algeria, Mauritania)

Crazy for you

The fourteenth day of Ramadan
I was crazy for you
They all watched as I fell under your spell.

What sorcerer can explain your magic
O girl with the figure like a lamp
That makes you flee from me so far.

I enjoin you by all the children in the world
By the men of God wherever they may be
Beautiful girl do not abandon me!

Restive horse

She: Boy, before meeting you
I was impatient
You thought I was fleeing you.

One thing was to know pleasure
And the other was clear:
For you I have accepted hurt.

But truly your spoiled pleasure
In the torrent has been swept away
Forbidden you is the way of goodness.

He: In the days when I was in love
I flirted with the rebels
For such was my life.

I had a spirited mount
Always panting
To gallop wildly.

Then I met your fine beauty
In every way agreeing with me
And my mount became restive.

At sunrise
I was black and blue
So if you truly love me then heal me!

Hard is the first night

The young girl
Applies henna between her tears.

Her bracelets jangle as she moves
Her necklace is fragrant with cloves.

Dear sisters
Hard is the first night!

LALA (Zambia)

Guess I'm fooled again

I'd cross over that river
But now our bridge is burnt —
I'll fall in and be food for the fish.

Girl, you're no good for me
But who's the wiser now?
Guess I'm fooled again.

O mercy me!
Who's the wiser?
Guess I'm fooled again.

MALAGASY (Madagascar)

Tell me how you love me!

— Tell me how you love me!

— I love you as I love rice.

— No, you do not love me!
You will eat me only when you are hungry.
So how do you love me?

— I love you as I love water.

— No, you do not love me!
Your sweat will wash away your love.
So how do you love me?

— I love you as I love my fine clothes.

— No, you don't love me!
If you fall into debt you will exchange me
And I will vanish from your memory.
So how do you love me?

— I love you as I love honey.

— No, you do not love me!
You leave the honeycomb when you eat.
So how do you love me?

— I love you as I love our Prince.

— Yes, you do love me!

— His presence leaves me awestruck,
A look from him leaves me shy.

— Yes, you truly love me!
My dreams have come true,
My searching is complete.

— I love you as I love my mother and father:
Alive in one home
Laid to rest in one wood.

Fig trees I planted

Fig trees I planted
Because I wanted you to come
Palma Christi I planted
Because I wanted you in my arms.

Like delicate silk you are difficult —
The moment it is loved it tangles
So when the earth turns on you
And the sky turns on you.

When summer turns to winter
And winter turns to spring
When husband and wife love each other not
Like brother and sister let them respect one another.

It is in our nature to part

Like east moving over west —
That is how they describe you
They say you'd have no desire
Me, I desire no one save you
Yet it is in our nature to part
Though while we live we'll love each other.

Miss Chatterbox

— Hey Miss Chatterbox, you didn't want to swim yesterday,
But today you went swimming?

— I went swimming not for you but for others.
I am a white twig tossed on the water
And whether I sink or float
They'll neither mock me nor judge me.

For it's with the one I love I'll go
Be it upstream or down
Be it to Imamo or Andrantsay.
I am a ribbon bound to a bird
I am a round-leaved mountain peanut stem
And should my man leave me for another, then I'll leave him
Yet three times he's tried to change me and never found my
equal.

Come swimming!

Come swimming! Come swimming!
And we will swim, there in the Water-of-Goodness
Come rub my back!
And as you rub, speak this blessing:
"O I bless you, sweet back!
May two not possess you nor three
But let you be mine alone, I who rub you.

And if I must share a lover with another
Then let her fall ill and long be weak
So she may be neither mine nor his.

And if my lover is mine only
Then let her not shiver with cold."
For when I go away, I pray often
When I return, I speak these blessings:
"O let me care for you, you before me here!"

MANDINKA (Senegal, Gambia)

Mandingo Woman

As I was sleeping late one night
A white woman woke me.
"Give me space," she said, "to lay me down."
I opened my eyes, and saw nothing
But her hair falling over her shoulders.
And I asked,
"Who are you?
Where do you come from?
What do you want?"
I had not finished asking questions
When I saw her weeping.

Her chest was trembling
Like the legs of a dancing woman.
I arose and sat by her side,
Asking, "What is the matter?"
Her answer came, "I am a woman.
Don't you recognize a woman?"
And I replied, "I know only a Mandingo woman.
A woman who is black-skinned as I am,
A woman whose teeth are as white as the moon,
A woman who plaits her hair like a Mandingo mat."

She said, "Then, change my colour to a Mandingo woman's
Because it is for the love of blackness
That I came here.
Because it is for the love of blackness
That I desire to plait my hair
It is because of my love of blackness
That I weep.

Colour me like a Mandingo woman
And I shall pound for you.
Colour me like a Mandingo woman,
And I shall fetch water at the well to wash you.
Colour me like a Mandingo woman,
And I'll dance the *Lenjeng Wo* till the sun sets in the west."

That was what the white woman told me.
So I thank God that I am black.
I thank God that I am a son of Mandingo.
I thank God that I am a son of Africa.

MBOSI (Congo)

The Beauty

She appeared in the distance, tall
As the lightning that brushes a high palm tree.

The soft noise of her supple legs
Is like the compact stir of boars bursting out.

The warm hue of her skin
Is like a nightowl's plumage eager to enter the forest.

Come, draw near!
That I may contemplate your figure.

Your legs so well formed —
Your legs trace the slenderness of the *okwele* tree,
Your face is calm and clear
Like the line of the horizon of a far-off forest.

The small space that separates your two breasts
Is beautiful like the wake of the *akanya* fish's fin,
The tips of your breasts shiver
As if you were soaked by the rain!

Your neck curves beautifully
Like a boa powerfully coiling high up an anthill,
Your neck is a young gazelle's,
The folds of your neck
Are like the smooth trunk of a palm tree!

Your sleepy eyes are small like lamprey eggs,
Your eyes are white, big and small, like eggs of the *ndzundza* bird.

Your teeth are pretty and small
Like stalks of straw,
Your belly is supple and smooth like a tender stem of
    asparagus.

And there she reclines on the bed,
Compact like a willow basket filled with salt,
Her body so perfect she floats in the air!

Us two!

Us two, poor us!
You and I
Alas!
Us two, poor us
Us two, truly
In what season will you return?
O child of others!
Take care of yourself! Lies are all around you
A baby elephant is carried on one's shoulders,
so precious it is
Who will I ask for news of you? —
To those who go and come on the roads?
To you, O youngest sister? —
My feet walk tirelessly on the highway
Who will I ask for news of you?
O woe is me!
Who will I ask for news of you?
My love
O child of others
You and I, heart to heart.

OROMO (Southern Ethiopia)

O autumn of the rains

O bag full of cotton
O flower flourish!
Oh autumn of the rains
O flower!
Come near me and dance
O flower!
O slender one, O beautiful one
O flower!
Let us join like the first rains
O flower!
And like the autumn of the rains . . .

SHONA (Zimbabwe)

LUKE C. CHIDAVAENZI

Our love by the river

Moontime, sun yellows down —
There the field, stubbled, bare,
We two together, sharing joy,
Walking, smiling-eyed, to the rushing river.

Leaving our home behind us
Sauntering, no rush, full of each other —
Close, we touch and touch, love kindled,
Passing us, our people, gently greeting.

Through the gaunt woods, across the drift hills,
We murmur softly — nearing the
Mhanyami river, now violent,
Rushing water lined with *horonga* willows.

Hitting the wet bank, looking down into pools so deep
There, where big boats ferry in summer,
Now, sweet-swaying willows, hanging
Over the foaming banks of reeds.

Talking, we talk, the words are sweet,
Our ears full of their honey, our eyes
Filling our faces, all love, and the water outside,
Inside all calm love, you and me, the easy cross-over.

In every place we are alone, but we want more,
So we walk on, following the coursing waters,
Our own currents cutting the channels deeper,
Our own moss and rocks and trees our inner landscape.

Then, so secure, handholding, watching the outer stream,
Our eyes tugged by the rush and push,
We search out, then gingerly step on the flat stones
Moving over the white spray of the mighty Mhanyami.

All the while we recalled our first days of love,
Calling back the streams of flowing love,
Floating still on the water's back with love,
Conjuring up the future of love, joined forever.

Sun was no friend, now eating the treetops
Doves and water birds seek the thick boughs for rest
Warned by the flutter, dimness on river, peacefully
We turn homewards, leaving the water for our own nest.

So, each day, my beloved, our shared love lives,
And our happy days on the river's edge flows in our hearts
These moments permanent in our memory, engraved in
our breasts
Breathe like eternal flowers, spring and summer till our
last fall.

SOMALI (Somalia)

SIRAAD XAAD

Lament for a dead lover

You were the fence standing between our land and
the descendants of Ali
Now in you departure you are the sky which gives
no rain while mist shrouds the world
The moon that shines no more
The risen sun extinguished
The dates on their way from Basra cut off by the seas.

Will I ever find your like?

You are the kilt a young dandy set out to choose
You are the fine ring for which thousands were paid
Will I ever find your like, you who have been shown to me
but once?
An umbrella that unfolds, yet you are as strong as looped iron
You who are as the gold of Nairobi, finely molded
You are the risen sun, and the early rays of dawn
Will I ever find your like, you who have been shown to me
only once?

XUSAYN AW FAARAX

Love that is is true

Trees are planted in the earth
So their roots are set below
If not they would surely fall
Such is the way they are
— And love that is true
Love that is is true
Shall never move from its place
For its centre is rooted firm in the ground.

Love is like the thickness
Of a treetrunk and its sap
Such loftiness and resilience
Are intertwined there
— And love that is true
Love that is is true
Shall never be split asunder
For it reaches right to the core.

Love is like a copse of willowy trees
That balance each other true
Each branch grows straight
Embracing the others by its side
— And love that is true
Love that is is true
Shall always share life's ways
Born faithful to each other.

Love is like the green grass
The shade of all the leaves
The colour of all the flowers
The hue of all the seeds
— And love that is true
Love that is is true

Is thunder and lightning
The rainclouds and their drops.

Love is like mistletoe
After is has encircled a branch
And entwined itself its length
Growing swiftly ever upward
— Once love is true for us
We cannot hide from on another
We can never hide from one another —
And then our dawn will turn to day.

SWAHILI (Kenya, Tanzania, Uganda, Zaire)

KALUTA AMRI ABEDI

Marry!

Marry don't marry an outcast whose looks lack manners
Marry don't marry the beauty scattered in her thoughts
Marry don't marry the pagan overproud and vulgar
Marry don't marry waywardness marry one who has our ways!

Marry she who takes you fancy beauty in body and soul
Marry the legitimate child knowledgeable of God's law
Marry the initiated maiden wise to the ways of womanhood
Marry don't marry waywardness marry one who has our ways!

Marry she of the same roots your mirror image indeed
Marry one of your rank of equal blood and breeding
Marry your uncle's daughter if perchance it happen
Marry don't marry waywardness marry one who has our ways!

Marry the beauty of beauties with aura pure and elegance
Marry a good and civil woman if you find yourself with one
Marry don't marry an extrovert a fire whose blaze you fan
Marry don't marry waywardness marry one who has our ways!

Marry treat her best of all the wife you come to choose
Marry be ever compassionate she should be always at her ease
Marry and give her respect even she who is flirtatious
Marry don't marry waywardness marry one who has our ways!

Marry she who has soft eyes which glisten and sparkle
Marry where you heart trusts she who will enrich you
Marry yes, she without blemish innocent and untouched
Marry don't marry waywardness marry one who has our ways!

Marry I tell you marry! try and try again
Marry and do so with care pray for her to Our Lord
Marry seek to settle down don't court wagging tongues
Marry don't marry waywardness marry one who has our ways!

Marry everything changes the world is spinning backwards
Marry never feel ashamed but be a better husband
Marry the way I write it down think of what I say
Marry don't marry waywardness marry one who has our ways!

Marry now I put a seal on this a good person brings a good end
Marry beware a bad person whose end is always drowning
Marry I command you, marry! for marriage brings you peace
Marry don't marry waywardness marry one who has our ways!

What once we had . . .

What once we had is now a trial
Our souls had fused together
But now it is such torture —
See what torture — to part.
Can you ever see why
We do one another harm.

All night long I toss and turn
Unable to sit for visions of you
Slowly going out of my mind
I call out to you by name
But no — it's only your shadow
And you are no longer mine alone.

The heat of our tongues
Which we so exchanged —
I cannot say another word!
Nor of all that we did together
Such things of wonder now
The like I've not seen since.

Like twins inseparable
We moved as one body —
O my love now you've left me
And now I've lost my life
From dawn to dusk I suffer
The sight of you my only cure.

The fig is the fruit of love

The fig is the fruit of love
To bestow upon a guest
It brings with it comfort too
And sets your cares to rest
But not for those who know not pleasure
For they shall debase it.

Distant is its sweetness
Difficult is its taste
It can make problems that poison it
Create a situation that spoils
And you shall gain no pleasure from it
Unless your mind is at ease.

O you who have tasted the fig
O you who have enjoyed it
Tell me if I speak untruth
Permit me not to lie
By God you shall not enjoy the fig
If you understand it not.

It shall not come to you easily
It is a fruit not easily shaken down
It may fall with the greatest crash
And its words will undress you
Then its shape may be quite different
From the good luck it was given.

Sunshine

Yours is the face of the sun
Light everlasting
Yours is the shape of joy
I dreamt you sent your hand back
There where you caressed me
O come again my dearest.

You have avoided me
You noble one
I have memories of joy
Your sunshine in the night
There where you caressed me
O come again my dearest.

I never stop shaking my head
Trying my sweet to hush you
To me yesterday feels like today
And in my heart you have risen
There where you caressed me
O come again my dearest.

Sunshine of mine to you I pray
A heart and all things good
I am tortured by you
My suffering will be ceaseless unless
There where you caressed me
You come again my dearest.

Matches and petrol

Matches and petrol
When you store them
These two things
Must never meet
Nothing would go right
And the whole place would explode
Far better to keep them apart
If peace is to prevail.

No, no peace will prevail
Of that you can be certain
Fire cannot be avoided
Of that you can be sure
Difficult then to quell
When the flames burst into life
Like her too I have a fire
From destruction there's no escape
Trust them at your peril
Never hesitate a second
Utterly incompatible
Primed to spark at once
You have no defense
And there's no one can help you
Of this you can be always sure —
That fire cannot be put out.

The rendezvous

The time you told me
My darling was not correct
I cannot agree that I delayed
Three quarters of an hour!
But you reproached me sharply
Such is your self-esteem.

Out of remorse I weep
Noble one, how I wish
That you would look inside me
And see how love compels me
Then you'd be gentle in your reproach
And forgive me here and now.

Appointments are sacred things
Of course they must be kept
Of that, esteemed lady, I speak true
The words of your servant ring true
So absolve me, see me kneel before you
My own words were untrue.

Don't be vexed, my sister
By these words I utter
For as long as you live
I'll never let you down
Though a raw wound I know
Is bound to keep on hurting.

African Love Poems

TIGRINYA (Eritrea)

ASGHEDOM W-MICHAEL

Asmeret

You whose eyes are like stars
    You walk so beautifully
You're like the rays of the setting sun
    As night is about to fall
Your silken hair and golden neck
    I'm drowning in your love.

Asmeret, Asmeret, life's sweetness
    O Asmeret, sweet as honey.

Enthroned in love you are
    You're as wise as you are beautiful
I'll spend my life with you if you'll let me
    As my heart cries out to you
Without shame I'm on my knees begging you
    Please — tell me that you will, Asmeret.

Asmeret, Asmeret, life's sweetness
    O Asmeret, sweet as honey.

I suffer with my every thought of you
    In the wind I hear your voice call me
I've made up my mind to be with you
    It's my heart's only option.
If you don't give me your answer true
    As the sun sets my life will lose its meaning.

Asmeret, Asmeret, life's sweetness
    O Asmeret, sweet as honey.

YORUBA (Nigeria)

Your daughter is beautiful, we love her!

Bridegroom's party: Your daughter is beautiful, we love her!
She is like a gazelle,
She is perfect beauty
She carries herself with such grace!

Bride's party: Our daughter is beautiful, you love her!
She the best of girls
She eats not bitter herbs
But dines on the finest of fish!

Both parties: O yesterday's bride!
She is like a gazelle,
A beautiful bride,
She carries herself with such grace!

ZULU (South Africa)

The body perishes

The body perishes, the heart stays young
The platter wears away with serving food
No log retains its bark when old
No lover peaceful while the rival weeps.

Love is blind

Tell me, friend, where is my love?
When I remember her, I feel an orphan
In this land of ours.
Had I but wings to fly to her —
Where is she, where my love? —
She would dispel my longing.
Hasten — it is eternal,
Love is blind.

Even while I long for her
Hope is never lost.
It is eternal.
What has gone before shall come again.
Where shall I go?
O woe! I die with love of her.
She would dispel my longing.
Help me . . . tell me where she is.
Love is blind.

Where is she,
Where, my love? —
She would dispel my longing.
O hasten!
It is eternal,
And love is blind.

With what will I wed her?

With what will I wed her?
I possess no cattle!
With what will I wed her?

You will never get her

So long as you see me walking,
Lost and alone,
So long as I live,
You will never get her!

American Love Poems

AMERICAN FOLK SONG

Frankie and Johnny

Frankie and Johnny were lovers,
Lordy , how they could love,
Swore to be true to each other,
True as the stars above,
He was her man, but he done her wrong.

Little Frankie was a good gal,
As everybody knows,
She did all the work around the house,
And pressed her Johnny's clothes,
He was her man, but he done her wrong.

Johnny was a yeller man,
With coal black, curly hair,
Everyone up in St. Louis
Thought he was a millionaire,
He was her man, but he done her wrong.

Frankie went down to the bar-room,
Called for a bottle of beer,
Says, "Looky here, Mister Bartender,
Has my lovin' Johnny been here?
He is my man, and he's doin' me wrong."

"I will not tell you no story,
I will not tell you no lie,
Johnny left here about an hour ago,
With a gal named Nelly Bly,
He is your man, and he's doing you wrong."

Little Frankie went down Broadway,
With her pistol in her hand,
Said, "Stand aside you chorus gals,
I'm lookin' for my man,
He is my man, and he's doin' me wrong."

The first time she shot him, he staggered,
The next time she shot him, he fell,
The last time she shot, O Lawdy,
There was a new man's face in hell,
She shot her man, for doin' her wrong.

"Turn me over doctor,
Turn me over slow,
I got a bullet in my left hand side,
Great God, it's hurtin' me so.
I was her man, but I done her wrong."

It was a rubber-tyred buggy,
Decorated hack,
Took poor Johnny to the graveyard,
Brought little Frankie back,
He was her man, but he done her wrong.

It was not murder in the first degree,
It was not murder in the third.
A woman simply dropped her man
Like a hunter drops his bird,
She shot her man, for doin' her wrong.

The last time I saw Frankie,
She was sittin' in the 'lectric chair,
Waitin' to go and meet her God
With the sweat runnin' out of her hair,
She shot her man, for doin' her wrong.

Walked on down Broadway,
As far as I could see,
All I could hear was a two string bow
Playin' *"Nearer my God to thee,"*
He was her man, and he done her wrong.

ANNE BRADSTREET (1612?–1672)

To My Dear and Loving Husband

If ever two were one, then surely we.
If ever man were lov'd by wife, then thee;
If ever wife was happy in a man,
Compare with me ye women if you can.
I prize thy love more than whole Mines of gold,
Or all the riches that the East doth hold.
My love is such that Rivers cannot quench,
Nor ought but love from thee, give recompence.
Thy love is such I can no way repay,
The heavens reward thee manifold I pray.
Then while we live, in love lets so persever,
That when we live no more, we may live ever.

PHILLIS WHEATLEY (1753?–1784)

To the Rev. Mr. Pitkin on the Death of His Lady

WHERE Contemplation finds her sacred Spring;
Where heav'nly Music makes the Centre ring;
Where Virtue reigns unsulled, and divine;
Where Wisdom thron'd, and all the Graces shine;
There sits thy Spouse, amid the glitt'ring Throng;
There central Beauty feasts the ravish'd Tongue;
With recent Powers, with recent glories crown'd,
The Choirs angelic shout her Welcome round.
The virtuous Dead, demand a grateful Tear —
But cease thy Grief a-while, thy Tears forbear,
Not thine alone, the Sorrow I relate,
Thy blooming Off-spring feel the mighty Weight;
Thus, from the Bosom of the tender Vine,
The Branches torn, fall, wither, sink supine.
Now flies the Soul, tho' Æther unconfin'd.
Thrice happy State of the immortal Mind!
Still in thy Breast tumultuous Passions rise,
And urge the lucent Torrent from thine Eyes.
Amidst the Seats of Heaven, a Place is free
For thee, they wait — and with expectant Eye,
Thy Spouse leans forward from th' ethereal Sky,
Thus in my Hearing, "Come away," she cries,
"Partake the sacred Raptures of the Skies!
"Our Bliss divine, to Mortals is unknown,
"And endless Scenes of Happiness our own;
"May the dear Off-spring of our earthly Love,
"Receive Admittance to the Joys above!

"Attune the Harp to more than mortal Lays,
"And pay with us, the Tribute of their Praise
"To Him, who died, dread Justice to appease,
"Which reconcil'd, holds Mercy in Embrace;
"Creation too, her MAKER'S Death bemoan'd,
"Retir'd the Sun, and deep the Centre groan'd.
"He in his Death slew ours, and as he rose,
"He crush'd the Empire of our hated Foes.
"How vain their Hopes to put the GOD to flight,
"And render Vengence to the Sons of Light!"
Thus having spoke she turn'd away her Eyes,
Which beam'd celestial Radiance o'er the Skies.
Let Grief no longer damp the sacred Fire,
But rise sublime, to equal Bliss aspire;
Thy Sighs no more be wafted by the Wind,
Complain no more, but to be Heav'n resign'd.
'Twas thine to shew those Treasure all divine,
To sooth our Woes, the Task was also thine.
Now Sorrow is recumbent on thy Heart,
Permit the Muse that healing to impart,
Nor can the World, a pitying tear refuse,
They weep, and with them, ev'ry heavenly Muse.

RALPH WALDO EMERSON (1803–1882)

Give All to Love

Give all to love;
Obey thy heart;
Friends, kindred, days,
Estate, good-fame,
Plans, credit and the Muse, —
Nothing refuse.

'Tis a brave master;
Let it have scope:
Follow it utterly,
Hope beyond hope:
High and more high
It dives into noon,
With wing unspent,
Untold intent;
But it is a god,
Knows its own path
And the outlets of the sky.

It was never for the mean;
It requireth courage stout.
Souls above doubt,
Valor unbending,
It will reward, —
They shall return
More than they were,
And ever ascending.

Leave all for love;
Yet, hear me, yet,
One word more thy heart behoved,
One pulse more of firm endeavor, —
Keep thee to-day,
Tomorrow, forever,
Free as an Arab
Of thy beloved.

Cling with life to the maid;
But when the surprise,
First vague shadow of surmise
Flits across her bosom young,
Of a joy apart from thee,
Free be she, fancy-free;
Nor thou detain her vesture's hem,
Nor the palest rose she flung
From her summer diadem.

Though thou loved her as thyself,
As a self of purer clay,
Though her parting dims the day,
Stealing grace from all alive;
Heartily know,
When half-gods go,
The gods arrive.

HENRY WADSWORTH LONGFELLOW (1807–1882)

The Fire of Drift-wood

We sat within the farm-house old,
  Whose windows, looking o'er the bay,
Gave to the sea-breeze damp and cold,
  An easy entrance, night and day.

Not far away we saw the port,
  The strange, old-fashioned, silent town,
The lighthouse, the dismantled fort,
  The wooden houses, quaint and brown.

We sat and talked until the night,
  Descending, filled the little room;
Our faces faded from the sight,
  Our voices only broke the gloom.

We spake of many a vanished scene,
  Of what we once had thought and said,
Of what had been, and might have been,
  And who was changed, and who was dead;

And all that fills the hearts of friends,
  When first they feel, with secret pain,
Their lives thenceforth have separate ends,
  And never can be one again;

The first slight swerving of the heart,
  That words are powerless to express,
And leave it still unsaid in part,
  Or say it in too great excess.

The very tones in which we spake
  Had something strange, I could but mark;
The leaves of memory seemed to make
  A mournful rustling in the dark.

Oft died the words upon our lips,
  As suddenly, from out the fire
Built of the wreck of stranded ships,
  The flames would leap and then expire.

And, as their splendor flashed and failed,
  We thought of wrecks upon the main,
Of ships dismasted, that were hailed
  And sent no answer back again.

The windows, rattling in their frames,
  The ocean, roaring up the beach,
The gusty blast, the bickering flames,
  All mingled vaguely in our speech;

Until they made themselves a part
  Of fancies floating through the brain,
The long-lost ventures of the heart,
  That send no answers back again.

O flames that glowed! O hearts that yearned!
  They were indeed too much akin,
The drift-wood fire without that burned,
  The thoughts that burned and glowed within.

EDGAR ALLAN POE (1809–1849)

A Dream Within a Dream

Take this kiss upon the brow!
And, in parting from you now,
Thus much let me avow —
You are not wrong, who deem
That my days have been a dream:
Yet if hope has flown away
In a night, or in a day,
In a vision, or in none,
Is it therefore the less *gone*?
All that we see or seem
Is but a dream within a dream.

I stand amid the roar
Of a surf-tormented shore,
And I hold within my hand
Grains of the golden sand —
How few! yet how they creep
Through my fingers to the deep,
While I weep — while I weep!
O God! can I not grasp
Them with a tighter clasp?
O God! can I not save
One from the pitiless wave?
Is *all* that we see or seem
But dream within a dream?

WALT WHITMAN (1819–1892)

A Glimpse

A glimpse through an interstice caught,
Of a crowd of workmen and drivers in a bar-room
around the stove late of a winter night, and I
unremark'd seated in a corner,
Of a youth who loves me and whom I love, silently
approaching and seating himself near, that he
may hold me by the hand,
A long while amid the noises of coming and going, of
drinking and oath and smutty jest,
There are two, content, happy in the being together,
speaking little, perhaps not a word.

EMILY DICKINSON (1830–1886)

With a Flower

I hide myself within a flower
That wearing on your breast,
You, unsuspecting, wear me too —
And angels know the rest.

I hide myself within my flower,
That, fading from your vase,
You, unsuspecting, feel for me
Almost a loneliness.

The Little Toil of Love

I had no time to hate, because
The grave would hinder me,
And life was not so ample I
Could finish enmity.

Nor had I time to love; but since
Some industry must be,
The little toil of love, I thought,
Was large enough for me.

THEODORE DREISER (1871–1945)

Love [I]

I stood in the rain
Outside that secret window
Where I knew she kept her tryst,
The window I was not supposed to know.
I knew she was there —
I saw her come to the front once,
A paper in her hand,
And sit and read.
Our child was with her, too —
Our child!
She told me they were going to Westchester.

And then I went back to our home to wait,
To tell her of her shame,
My hate,
To drive her out,
To mourn,
To curse,
To say that I had seen,
To say that she had lied.

Yet when she came,
Cold, brave and desirable,
How well I know,
That if I spoke
Or raged
She would then leave
Would never more return —
And so
I
Who desired to scorn
To strike
To slay —

I gulped my rage,
The hate that in me stormed,
The misery —
And smiled,
So covering my madness with a smile.
"Bessie," I said,
"And was your visit pleasant?"
Yet all the while I was a-cold with rage.
I hated,
Groaned.
That night, alone, I strode the streets
And sobbed,
And once (believe it) vomited,
So sore was I at heart.
My business needing me,
I still walked on
That day
And others,
Walking, walking long
And never knowing peace.
And yet,
In time,
She left me anyhow,
My arts to no avail.
But still the pain is here,
Is still in my heart,
My groin,
And it is twenty years.

THEODORE DREISER

Love Plaint

I have sought to fetter love, —
To bind it.
But love is like a the wind
Stirring in the tall grass at night
Under great trees
In the dark.
It may not be seen
Or fettered
But only felt.
Or,
Again,
Love is like a distant voice
On sea or land,
In fog or storm
That calls and calls
And speaks of need.
A sweet voice that would give.
Or love is like a perfume
That the wind brings
But that one cannot place
Or know, —
A rumor of old things that were
Or yet may be
Or are,
But that one may not hold.
It dwells where shadow is
And song
And dream,
And sings
Or weeps
Or calls
And, oh, the ache
Of that elusive call.

But I, —
I sought to bind love
And it fled.
And now the searing day has come, —
The blare and crash of life, —
The long hot day of want —
And now the grit and dust
Of life's hard, thundering wheels
Are on my lips
And in my eyes
Inflamed and yet made tender
By Love's lips.

PAUL LAURENCE DUNBAR (1872–1906)

A Negro Love Song

Seen my lady home las' night,
  Jump back honey, jump back.
Hel' huh han' an' sque'z it tight,
  Jump back honey, jump back.
Heahd huh sigh a little sigh,
Seen a light gleam f'um huh eye,
An' a smile go flitin' by —
  Jump back honey, jump back.

Heahd de win' blow thoo de pines,
  Jump back honey, jump back.
Mockin' bird was singin, fine,
  Jump back honey, jump back.
An' my hea't was beatin' so,
When I reached my lady's do',
Dat I couldn't ba' to go —
  Jump back, honey, jump back.

Put my ahm aroun' huh wais',
  Jump back, honey, jump back.
Raised huh lips an took a tase',
  Jump back, honey, jump back.
Love me honey, love me true?
Love me well ez I love you?
An' she ansawhd: "'Cose I do" —
  Jump back, honey, jump back.

ROBERT FROST (1874–1963)

The Investment

Over back where they speak of life as staying
("You couldn't call it living, for it ain't"),
There was an old, old house renewed with paint,
And in it a piano loudly playing.

Out in the ploughed ground in the cold a digger,
Among unearthed potatoes standing still,
Was counting winter dinners, one a hill,
With half an ear to the piano's vigor.

All that piano and a new paint back there,
Was it some money suddenly come into?
Or some extravagance young love had been to?
Or old love on an impulse not to care —

Not to sink under being man and wife
But get some color and music out of life?

WILLIAM CARLOS WILLIAMS (1883–1963)

Portrait of a Lady

Your thighs are appletrees
whose blossoms touch the sky.
Which sky? The sky
where Watteau hung a lady's
slipper. Your knees
are a southern breeze — or
a gust of snow. Agh! what
sort of man was Fragonard?
— as if that answered
anything. Ah, yes — below
the knees, since the tune
drops that way, it is
one of those white summer days,
the tall grass of your ankles
flickers upon the shore —
Which shore? —
the sand clings to my lips —
Which shore?
Agh, petals maybe. How
should I know?
Which shore? Which shore?
I said petals from an appletree.

SARA TEASDALE (1884–1933)

After Parting

Oh I have sown my love so wide
That he will find it everywhere;
It will awake him in the night,
It will enfold him in the air.

I set my shadow in his sight
And I have singed it with desire,
That it may be a cloud by day
And in the night a shaft of fire.

The Look

Strephon kissed me in the spring,
 Robin in the fall,
But Colin only looked at me
 And never kissed at all.

Strephon's kiss was lost in jest,
 Robin's lost in play,
But the kiss in Colin's eyes
 Haunts me night and day.

The Years

To-night I close my eyes and see
A strange procession passing me —
The years before I saw your face
Go by me with a wistful grace;
They pass, the sensitive shy years,
As one who strives to dance, half blind with tears.

The years went by and never knew
That each one brought me nearer you;
Their path was narrow and apart
And yet it led me to your heart —
Oh sensitive shy years, oh lonely years,
That strove to sing with voices drowned in tears.

JOHN CROWE RANSOM (1888–1974)

Parting Without a Sequel

She has finished and sealed the letter
At last, which he so richly deserved,
With characters venomous and hatefully curved,
And nothing could be better.

But even as she gave it,
Saying to the blue-capped functioner of doom,
'Into his hands,' she hoped the leering groom
Might somewhere lose and leave it.

Then all the blood
Forsook the face. She was too pale for tears,
Observing the ruin of her younger years.
She went and stood

Under her father's vaunting oak
Who kept his peace in wind and sun, and glistened
Stoical in the rain; to whom she listened
If he spoke.

And now the agitation of the rain
Rasped his sere leaves, and he talked low and gentle,
Reproaching the wan daughter by the lintel;
Ceasing, and beginning again.

Away went the messenger's bicycle,
His serpent's track went up the hill forever,
And all the time she stood there hot as fever
And cold as any icicle.

CONRAD AIKEN (1889–1973)

The Quarrel

Suddenly, after the quarrel, while we waited,
Disheartened, silent, with downcast looks, nor stirred
Eyelid nor finger, hopeless both, yet hoping
Against all hope to unsay the sundering word:

While all the room's stillness deepened, deepened about us,
And each of us crept his thought's way to discover
How, with as little sound as the fall of a leaf,
The shadow had fallen, and lover quarreled with lover;

And while, in the quiet, I marveled — alas, alas —
At your deep beauty, your tragic beauty, torn
As the pale flower is torn by the wanton sparrow —
This beauty, pitied and loved, and now forsworn;

It was then, when the instant darkened to its darkest, —
When faith was lost with hope, and the rain conspired
To strike its gray arpeggios against our heartstrings, —
When love no longer dared, and scarcely desired:

It was then that suddenly, in the neighbor's room,
The music started: that brave quartette of strings
Breaking out of the stillness, as out of our stillness,
Like the indomitable heart of life that sings

When all is lost; and startled from our sorrow,
Tranced from our grief by that diviner grief,
We raised remembering eyes, each looked at other,
Blinded with tears of joy; and another leaf

Fell silently as that first; and in the instant
The shadow had gone, our quarrel became absurd;
And we rose, to the angelic voices of the music,
And I touched your hand, and we kissed, without a word.

EDNA ST. VINCENT MILLAY (1892–1950)

Ebb

I know what my heart is like
Since your love died:
It is like a hollow ledge
Holding a little pool
Left there by the tide,
A little tepid pool,
Drying inward from the edge.

EDNA ST. VINCENT MILLAY

Recuerdo

We were very tired, we were very merry —
We had gone back and forth all night on the ferry,
It was bare and bright, and smelled like a stable —
But we looked into a fire, we leaned across a table,
We lay on a hill-top underneath the moon;
And the whistles kept blowing, and the dawn came soon.

We were very tired, we were very merry —
We had gone back and forth all night on the ferry;
And you ate an apple, and I ate a pear,
From a dozen of each we had brought somewhere;
And the sky went wan, and the wind came cold,
And the sun rose dripping, a bucketful of gold.

We were very tired, we were very merry —
We had gone back and forth all night on the ferry.
We hailed, "Good-morrow, mother!" to a shawl-covered head,
And bought a morning paper, which neither of us read;
And she wept, "God bless you!" for the apples and pears,
And we gave her all our money but our subway fares.

ARCHIBALD MacLEISH (1892–1982)

"Not Marble, Nor the Gilded Monuments"

The praisers of women in their proud and beautiful poems
Naming the grave mouth and the hair and the eyes
Boasted those they loved should be forever remembered
These were lies

The words sound but the face in the Istrian sun is forgotten
The poet speaks but to her dead ears no more
The sleek throat is gone — and the breast that was troubled
to listen
Shadow from door

Therefore I will not praise your knees nor your fine walking
Telling you men shall remember your name as long
As lips move or breath is spent or the iron of English
Rings form a tongue

I shall say you were young and your arms straight and your
mouth scarlet
I shall say you will die and none will remember you
Your arms change and none remember the swish of your
garments
Nor the click of your shoe

Not with my hand's strength not with difficult labor
Springing the obstinate words to the bones of your breast
And the stubborn line to your young stride and the breath to
your breathing
And the beat to your haste
Shall I prevail on the hearts of unborn men to remember

(What is a dead girl but a shadowy ghost
Or a dead man's voice but a distant and vain affirmation
Like dream words most)

Therefore I will not speak of the undying glory of women
I will say you were young and straight and your skin fair
And you stood in the door and the sun was shadow of leaves
    on your shoulders
And a leaf on your hair
I will not speak of the famous beauty of dead women
I will say the shape of a leaf lay once on your hair
Till the world ends and the eyes are out and the mouths
    broken
Look! It is there!

DOROTHY PARKER (1893–1967)

De Profundis

Oh, is it, then, Utopian
To hope that I may meet a man
Who'll not relate, in accents suave,
The tales of girls he used to have?

General Review of the Sex Situation

Woman wants monogamy;
Man delights in novelty.
Love is woman's moon and sun;
Man has other forms of fun.
Woman lives but in her lord;
Count to ten, and man is bored.
With this the gist and sum of it,
What earthly good can come of it?

E. E. CUMMINGS (1894–1962)

Somewhere I Have Never Travelled, Gladly Beyond

somewhere i have never travelled, gladly beyond
any experience, your eyes have their silence;
in your most frail gesture are things which enclose me,
or which i cannot touch because they are too near

Your slightest look easily will unclose me
though i have closed myself as fingers,
you open always petal by petal myself as Spring opens
(touching skilfully, mysteriously) her first rose

or if your wish be to close me, i and
my life will shut very beautifully, suddenly,
as when the heart of this flower imagines
the snow carefully everywhere descending;

nothing which we are to perceive in this world equals
the power of your intense fragility: whose texture
compels me with the colour of its countries,
rendering death and forever with each breathing

(i do not know what it is about you that closes
and opens; only something in me understands
the voice of your eyes is deeper than all roses)
nobody, not even the rain, has such small hands

OGDEN NASH (1902–1971)

I Never Even Suggested It

I know lots of men who are in love and lots of men who are married and lots of men who are both,
And to fall out with their loved ones is what all of them are most loth.
They are conciliatory at every opportunity,
Because all they want is serenity and a certain amount of impunity.
Yes, many the swain who has finally admitted that the earth is flat
Simply to sidestep a spat,
Many the masculine Positively or Absolutely which has been diluted to an If
Simply to avert a tiff,
Many the two-fisted executive whose domestic conversation is limited to a tactfully interpolated Yes,
And then he is amazed to find that he is being raked backwards over a bed of coals nevertheless.
These misguided fellows are under the impression that it takes two to make a quarrel, that you can sidestep a crisis by nonaggression and nonresistance,
Instead of removing yourself to a discreet distance.
Passivity can be a provoking *modus operandi*;
Consider the Empire and Gandhi.
Silence is golden, but sometimes invisibility is golder.
Because loved ones may not be able to make bricks without straw but often they don't need any straw to manufacture a bone to pick or blood in their eye or a chip for their soft white shoulder.
It is my duty, gentlemen, to inform you that women are dictators all, and I recommend to you this moral:
In real life it takes only one to make a quarrel.

KENNETH PATCHEN (1911–1972)

Fall of the Evening Star

Speak softly; sun going down
Out of sight. Come near me now.

Dear dying fall of wings as birds
Complain against the gathering dark . . .

Exaggerate the green blood in grass;
The music of leaves scraping space;

Multiply the stillness by one sound;
By one syllable of your name . . .

And all that is little is soon giant,
All that is rare grows in common beauty

To rest with my mouth on your mouth
As somewhere a star falls

And the earth takes it softly, in natural love . . .
Exactly as we take each other . . . and go to sleep

JOHN CIARDI (1916–1985)

To Judith Asleep

My dear, darkened in sleep, turned from the moon
That riots on curtain-stir with every breeze
Leaping in moths of light across your back . . .
Far off, then soft and sudden as petals shower
Down from wired roses — silently, all at once —
You turn, abandoned and naked, all let down
In ferny streams of sleep and petaled thighs
Rippling into my flesh's buzzing garden.

Far and familiar your body's myth-map lights,
Traveled by moon and dapple. Sagas were curved
Like scimitars to your hips. The raiders' ships
All sailed to your one port. And watchfires burned
Your image on the hills. Sweetly you drown
Male centuries in your chiaroscuro tide
Of breast and breath. All all my memory's shores
You frighten perfectly, washed familiar and far.

Ritual wars have climbed your shadowed flank
Where bravos dreaming of fair women tore
Rock out of rock to have your cities down
In loot of hearths and trophies of desire.
And desert monks have fought your image back
In a hysteria of mad skeletons.
Bravo and monk (the heads and tails of love)
I stand, a spinning coin of wish and dread,

Counting our life, our chairs, our books and walls,
Our clock whose radium eye and insect voice
Owns all our light and shade, and your white shell
Spiraled in moonlight on the bed's white beach;
Thinking, I might press you to my ear
And all your coils fall out in sounds of surf

Washing away our chairs, our books and walls,
Our bed and wish, our ticking light and dark.

Child, child, and making legend of my wish
Fastened alive into your naked sprawl —
Stir once to stop my fear and miser's panic
That time shall have you last and legendry
Undress to old bones from its moon brocade.
Yet sleep and keep our prime of time alive
Before that death of legend. My dear of all

Sage and century, sleep in familiar-far.
Time still must tick *this is, I am, we are.*

GWENDOLYN BROOKS (b. 1917)

love note I: surely

Surely you stay my certain own, you stay
My you. All honest, lofty as a cloud.
Surely I could come now and find you high,
As mine as you ever were; should not be awed.
Surely your word would pop as insolent
As always: "Why, of course I love you, dear."
Your gaze, surely, ungauzed as I could want.
Your touches, that never were careful, what they were.
Surely — But I am very off from that.
From surely. From indeed. From the decent arrow
That was my clean naïveté and my faith.
This morning men deliver wounds and death.
They will deliver death and wounds tomorrow.
And I doubt all. You. Or a violet.

love note II: flags

Still, it is dear defiance now to carry
Fair flags of you above my indignation,
Top, with a pretty glory and a merry
Softness, the scattered pound of my cold passion.
I pull down my foxhole. Do you mind?
You burn in bits of saucy color then.
I let you flutter out against the pained
Volleys. Against my power crumpled and wan.
You, and the yellow pert exuberance
Of dandelion days, unmocking sun:
The blowing of clear wind in your gay hair;
Love changeful in you (like a music, or
Like a sweet mournfulness, or like a dance,
Or like the tender struggle of a fan).

Arabic Love Poems

THE POET BASSĀR (711–782 A.D.)

Mukhtarat I

O my night, you grow ever more hateful, because of love I bear
towards a maiden with whom I have become enamoured.
A sparkling-eyed maiden is she; if she glances towards you,
she makes you drunk with wine by those two eyes.
The pattern of her discourse seems like meadow plots
garbed in flowers,
and as though beneath her tongue,
Harut sat breathing spells therein.
You might well imagine the body on which she gathers her
garments
to be all gold and scent.
It is as though she were the very coolness of drink itself —
drink pure and suited to your breaking fast.
Be she a maiden of the jinn, a human girl,
or somewhat between, she is a most splendid thing.
It is enough to say that I never heard tell of any complaint
about the one I love,
Save the cry of one who would visit her:
'She has scattered sorrows all around for me,
Victim of passion for a ten-day space,
and of very death for ten.'

Mukhatarat II

You two cupbearers, pour out my drink, and give me a draught
of the moist lips of a delicate fair maiden;

My sickness is thirst, my remedy
a drink from a cool moist mouth.

She has a smile like the shinning petals of the camomile,
a speech like embroidery, the embroidery of cloaks.

She has settled in the inmost recesses of my heart's core,
and has won even more than that, like one importunate.

Then she said, 'We will meet you some nights hence':
but the passage of nights will wear out every new thing.

She can rest content without meeting me:
but my lot is sighs which eat away a heart of iron.

ABU NUWAS AL-HASAN AL-HAKAMI (762–814 A.D.)

Banan's Face

Banan's face is like a moon
    Shining on a month's third night
A cheek in its beauty and glow
    Like a rose bouquet with its thorns
An air comes from her forehead
    Telling of the wild cow's sweet urine
A mouth when it smiles narrowly
    Is like a food tray set for the poor.

Her teeth tell of her brilliance
    And her beauty like balanced tongues
Beauty enough in her braids
    Like date clusters on their stalks
A fine neck for one who sees it
    Similar to the neck of the dragon
Her shoulders in their good shape
    Are like pomegranates among the figs
And belly folds whose softness tell
    Of what they conceal in doctors' books
Legs on whose softness are anklets
    As if they were pokers to stir a furnace.

She enchants one who looks at her
    with a glance whose look is criminal
The finest eye sockets among men
    Something like the whale's eye sockets
Nearest of humans to a snake's glide
    Its step is from Nasa all the way to China
You were born from a blessed clan
    No stain was in it . . . from the Satans.

The Bearer of Love

The bearer of love tires
    And passion belittles him
If he wept it was due him
    His trouble was no joke to him
You laughed kindly
    But the beloved lamented
You wondered at my ills
    But my health was the wonder
Each time a bond broke
    Through you a new bond came.

I burn in two fires of her love, one
    Is on her cheeks, the other in my belly
I hold my tongue lest I make it known
    And nothing but my gesture interprets for me
O my folk, I was away before their eyes
    On my bed and they do not know what ails me
If your worldly rigor were as your rigor
    Toward my love you'd walk, no doubt, on water.

GIBRAN KHALIL GIBRAN (1883–1931)

Of Love

Sage:

Now should you meet a lover lost, bewildered, yet avoiding guide,
Disdaining though he thirsts to drink, in his own hunger satisfied;
Hear people say, "This youth bewitched what seek he from love so great?
What hope has he to patiently await his Kismet and his Fate?
Why waste his bloodstained tears for one
Who lacks all beauty and respect?"
Say of them all, they ate stillborn,
Know naught of life, nor can reflect.

Youth:

In the woods no blame attaches
To lover's tryst, nor watchers spy;
When a gazelle, ranging swiftly,
Greets its lovemate with a cry,
Eagles never display wonder,
Or say, "Tis marvel of the ages."
For in nature we the children
Only hold the sane as strange.

Al-Mahabah

Then said Almitra, Speak to us of Love.
And he raised his head and looked upon the people, and there fell a stillness upon them. And with a great voice he said:
When love beckons to you, follow him,
Though his ways are hard and steep.
And when his wings enfold you yield to him,
Though the sword hidden among his pinions may wound you.
And when he speaks to you believe in him,
Though his voice may shatter your dreams as the north wind lays waste the garden.

For even as love crowns you
so shall he crucify you.
Even as is for your growth
so is he for your pruning.
Even as he ascends to your height and caresses your tenderest branches
that quiver in the sun,
So shall he descend to your roots and shake them in their clinging to the earth.

Like sheaves of corn he gathers you unto himself.
He threshes you to make you naked.
He sifts you to free you from your husks.
He grinds you to whiteness.
He kneads you until you are pliant:
And then he assigns you to his sacred fire,
that you may become sacred bread for God's sacred feast.

All these things shall love do unto you
that you may know the secrets of your heart,
and in that knowledge become a fragment of life's heart.

But if in your fear you should seek only
love's peace and love's pleasure,
Then it is better for you that you cover
your nakedness and pass out of love's threshing-floor,
Into the seasonless world where you
shall laugh, but not all of your laughter,
and weep, but not all of your tears.

Love gives naught but itself and takes
naught but from itself.
Love possesses not nor would it be possessed;
For love is sufficient unto love.

When you love you should not say,
"God is in my heart, "but rather, "I am
in the heart of God".
And think not you can direct the course
of love, for love, if it finds you worthy,
directs your course.
Love has no other desire but to fulfill itself.
But if you love and must needs have
desire, let these be your desires:
To melt and be like a running brook
that sings its melody to the night.
To know the pain of too much tenderness.
To be wounded by your own understanding of love;
And to bleed willingly and joyfully.
To wake at dawn with winged heart
and give thanks for another day of loving;
To rest at the noon hour and mediate love's ecstasy;
To return home at eventide with gratitude;
And then sleep with a prayer for the
beloved in your heart and song of praise upon your lips.

`IBRAHIM `ABD AL-QADIR AL-MAZINI (1890–1949)

The Wilted Rose

Fragrance like your lover's breaths
   when her mouth comes near you.
And dried up land, the clouds passed by
   with heavy rains until he quenched her thirst.
It wilted and her beauty was more natural
   would God! If only my poetry didn't make her clever.
I watered her with my tears —
   if possible to make her live, it would have
And I embrace her in the lover's embrace
   perhaps her youth will return to her.
And I moaned so perhaps my moaning
   will help, but wilted even more
And I threw her against my
   will, I am the one that threw her.
And if I could, I would bend
   my ribs on her wilted splendor
And I would make my chest her grave
   and I would make my intestines her soil.

`IBRAHIM NAJI (1898–1953)

The Burning Flute

How many times my love
as the night covers the earth
I wander alone, and in the dark
no one complains but me.
I make the tears a tune
and I make the poetry a flute
And would a wreck responds
that I inflamed in my ardent love.
Fire stirs in it
and the wind blows away the rest.
How miserable is the flute between
destiny and between fates
He sings and sadly sings
returning my complaints.
Sympathetic from our kept secrets
on the love of innermost secrets
Until a shadow appears.
I have known him in my youth
He comes close to me and he comes close
to the lips of my mouth
And suddenly my dreams disappears
and my eyes wake up
And though I went listening and listening
I wasn't familiar but with the echo.

AMAL DUNQUL (1940–1982)

Oh . . . Her Face

Love wished us to meet . . . inadvertently
how I used to miss you
oh her pretty face.

All that I named: Chanted
from before I found you;
dawned on the lips of youth . . . foolish talk.

Be for me as I love
warmth and beauty rained on me
and my hands spread your elevated worries
and your fertile ground moaned.

Oh when I promise you
the summer in your embrace the awakening.
Your eyes get loose in a swing
and your mouth trembles with no shelter
and his torment: Consolation
if I came to shake his complaint.

At night I miss you
your intoxicated features light up to me
you come proudly shamed of disclosure
and I lean you against the arm of longing
and I feel in my face the blazing breaths
when your comfort wraps me!
and I sleep.
Seeing you carries me to a distant star
we step gently,
we talk, and I sip your loose whispers
that awaken me shaking . . . so I miss you
but with no use
with no use!

Oh her pretty face
rains, as I am barren of consolation
I still don't have the strength
to move my steps
if I missed you leaning.

Oh her pretty face
I still miss you
I still miss you.

The Green Eyes

The green eyes,
two propellers,
in the verandas of the hot summer.
Two traveling songs
sailed from the shepards' flutes
in a tender fragrance
with a consolation from the Gods of light to the cities
of sadness.
Two years
and I have been building the boat of love.
Extends on it two sails of longing
so I can sail in the clear eyes
to the coral islands.
How sweet when the waves are unsettled so the eyelids drop
and I am searching for an oar for faith
in the silence of the splendoring cathedrals.

Pictures of the "virgin" with the lowered eyelids
you who breast-fed love of forgiveness prayer
and you mounted in your lowered eyes
the youth of deprivation.
Roll over your eyelids . . .
Are they green
like the eyes of my love?
Like the eyes that the sea sails in with no shores
asking about love
about my memory
about forgetting?
My heart is heated, heated
and the green eyes
are propellers.

Chinese Love Poems

HSÜ CHIH-MO (1895–1931)

Late At Night

Late at night, around the street corner,
A dreamlike bloom of lamplight.

Mist bewitches and shrouds the tree;
No wonder people lose their way.

"What have you done to me — you cruel thing!"
She weeps; he — no answer.

The morning breeze rocks the treetop gently,
Gone is the red blossom in early autumn.

The Joy of The Snowflake

If I were a snowflake,
Drifting freely in the sky,
   I'd make sure of my direction —
   To fly, and fly, and fly —
There is a direction for me on earth.

I won't go to the lonely sequestered vale,
I won't go to the foothill so quiet and cool,
   Nor shall I loiter sadly in a deserted street —
   I'll just fly, and fly, and fly —
You see, I have my direction.

Gracefully I shall dance in the sky
Until I've spotted that pleasant place,
   Until she comes out to see the garden —
   I'll fly, and fly, and fly —
Ah, there is a subtle scent of the plum blossom on her.

Then I'll count on my body being so light
Gently I'll cling to the lapel of her robe,
   I'll cling close to the soft waves of her bosom —
   To melt away, and melt away, and melt away —
Melt into the soft waves of her bosom.

A P'i-pa Tune in an Alley at Midnight

Again waking me up from a dream, a tune of p'i-pa in the still of the night!
Whose sorrowful thought,
And whose fingers,
Like a gust of chilly wind, a spell of depressing rain, and a shower of falling petals,
So late at night,
In so drowsy a world,
Are strumming the taut chords to send forth these disturbing notes
To blend into the night in the deserted street,
While a waning moon hangs on top of a willow tree?
Ah, the sliver of a moon, a shattered hope, and he, he . . .
Wearing a tattered cap,
With clanking chains on his back,
Laughs and dances on the path of time like a mad soul.
That's all, he says, blow out our lamp,
She is waiting for you beyond her grave,
Waiting for you to kiss her, to kiss her again, and again.

CHU TA-NAN

Eviction

Since you moved in to live in my heart,
Disquietude is the rent you have been paying me.
I long for the day when there will be serenity:
Without your song and dance, my heart will be free.

When did I ever put up a "For Rent" notice?
All my life I have loved only void and quiet.
Get out, unwelcome intruder,
You sing and dance without stop, day and night.

My heart cannot bear this disturbance,
Your dance's rumble and your noisy shout.
Get away, don't pretend to be silly;
One day I will serve notice and chase you out.

FANG WEI-TEH (d. 1935)

I Have

I have a thought
As I walk past you;
Like a mountain stream,
It's neither love nor attachment.

I have a thought
As I walk home;
Like a touch of afterglow
It's neither sorrow nor dejection.

WANG TU-CH'ING (1898–1940)

A Faded Rose

Under a pale green lamp I gaze at her,
I gaze at her light golden hair,
Her rougeless cheeks, her eyes blue and clear,
Ah, under a lamp of pale green color.

She gathered in her hands a pile of rose petals,
Bending her head, she kissed them again and again,
She offered them to me and told me
To hold them close to my lips as did she.

Ah, roses — I thanked them secretly:
You brought so close to me the scent of her hair,
You mingled our breaths in your own sweet remains
And your sweet remains sealed a kiss of ours.

Because in you our breaths are forever entombed,
Ah, roses, I wish to hold your sweet remains forever.
— I wish to keep this pale green lamp always,
And always sit this way, always next to her.

WEN I-TO (1899–1946)

Champion

O my love, you are a champion;
But let's play a game of chess.
My aim is not to win,
I wish only to lose to you —
My body and soul,
Both in their entirety.

Forget Her

Forget her, as a forgotten flower —
  That ray of morning sun on a petal
  That whiff of fragrance from a blossom —
Forget her, as a forgotten flower.

Forget her, as a forgotten flower,
  As a dream in a wind of spring,
  As in a dream, a bell's ring.
Forget her, as a forgotten flower.

Forget her, as a forgotten flower.
  Listen, how sweetly the crickets sing;
  Look, how tall the grass has grown.
Forget her, as a forgotten flower.

Forget her, as a forgotten flower.
  No longer does she remember you.
  Nothing now lingers in her memory.
Forget her, as a forgotten flower.

Forget her, as a forgotten flower.
  Youth, what a charming friend,
  Who makes you old overnight.
Forget her, as a forgotten flower.

Forget her, as a forgotten flower.
  If anyone should ask,
  Tell him she never existed.
Forget her, as a forgotten flower.

Forget her, as a forgotten flower.
  As a dream in the wind of spring,
  As in a dream, a bell's ring.
Forget her, as a forgotten flower.

LI CHIN-FA (b. 1900?)

Expression of Time

1

Wind and rain on the ocean,
Dead deer in my heart.
Look, autumn dream has left on spread wings
Only this dejected soul remains.

2

I pursue abandoned desires,
I mourn discolored lips.
Ah, on the shadowy grassland
The moon gathers our silence.

3

In the ancient palace of love,
Our honeymoon took ill and fell;
Take a half-burned candle, hurry,
Dusk is spreading over the fields and hills.

4

What do I want at this moment?
I seem to fear being scorched to death in the sun.
Go away, the garden gate is open,
And bees have entered on filmy slippers.

5

I await the wakening from a dream,
I await the sleep of a wakeful day:
With your tears in my eyes,
I cannot look back into the past.

6

You lean on a snowbank, thinking of spring,
I listen to the cicadas in withering grass;
Our lives are barren and laid waste,
Like a rice field in the wake of a stampede.

7

I sing folk tunes unrhymed.
With my heart keeping the beat,
Trust your sorrow, then, to my bosom
Where it will find its cure.

8

A lotus in the shade,
Cannot understand the brilliance of the sun and the moon,
Row your boat into the secluded pond,
To let the blossom learn a bit of the love of man.

9

Our memories
Are searching for their way home from the wilderness.

Tenderness

My fingers rude and crude
Touch the warmth of your skin;
The little fawn lost its way in the forest,
There is only the sound of dead leaves.

Your low whisper
Resounds in my barren heart.
A conqueror of all, I
Have broken my spear and shield.

Your eyes cast a glance,
Cast a butcher's warning;
Your lips? No need to mention them,
I'd rather trust your arms.

I believe in the fantasy of fairy tales,
But not in a woman's sentiment.
(Ah, making comparisons is not my habit.)
But you really resemble the shepherdess in a story.

I played all the tunes,
But nothing pleased your ear;
All colors have been exhausted,
Yet nothing can describe you beauty.

WANG CHING-CHIH (b. 1903)

Untitled

Sorrow is the unbounded sky,
  And happiness, the stars.
My love, you and I are
  The bright moon in the starry sea.

The deep roots are sorrow,
  And the green foliage, joy.
My love, those blooms growing on top
  Are you and I.

Water in the sea is joy,
  The unbounded sea itself, sorrow.
The fish swimming in the sea
  Are you and I, my love.

Sorrow is the countless bee hives,
  Joy, the sweet honey:
My love, you and I are the bees
  Working so busily.

TAI WANG-SHU (1905–1950?)

A Sonnet

Light rain fell on your unkempt hair:
So many little pearls sprinkled in black kelp,
So many dead fish tossed about on the waves,
With a mysterious, sad gleam

Luring and bringing my cheerless soul
To retire to the dreamland of love and death
Where purple sunshine lights up the golden air,
And pitiful creatures, unrestrained, weep happy tears.

Like a black cat, so old and thin,
I shall wither away and yawn in that soft twilight,
Pouring forth all my pride, both false and true;
Then I shall follow that mysterious gleam to stumble
In the hazy twilight, like a bubble of rosy wine floating in an
    amber glass,
Letting my sentimental eyes hide in the dark, murky memory.

FENG CHIH (b. 1905)

Sonnet III

You, a tree rustling in autumn winds
Are a movement of music that builds
A solemn temple near my ears
To let me enter with care;

You are also a tower piercing the sunny sky,
Rising majestically in front of me,
The body of a saint
Sublimating the noises of the whole city.

You never cease shedding your physical shell,
And in your withering one sees only your growth;
On the fields crisscrossed by narrow paths
I regard you as my guide.
Wishing you a life eternal: I'd like, little by little,
To change myself into the soil beneath your roots.

SUN YÜ-T'ANG (b. 1905?)

Complaint

Yes, you loved me, just for that wink of an eye —
Like a swallow's wing-tip touching the water,
A whiff of gentle breeze, leaving no shadow to be caught,
No light to be traced — like the flash of a falling star —

It was gone, You did not mind at all,
But unthinking, untied my anchor chain.
Thus on white sails, swollen with warm dreams,
I flew out of a river, across the sea, and soared over the hills,

Through blue clouds I darted into the depth of night,
Losing myself, and missing my road;
All because I took that instant to be eternity,
Thinking that the silver stars were your eyes.

Then you laughed, and that awakened me,
Awakened me to my earlier hasty belief.
But, ah, what do you want me to do now?
Now that you have slammed shut forever the door of
my paradise.

LI KUANG-T'IEN (b. 1907)

A Falling Star

A falling star, falling,
And falling with it
Are tears.

Thinking of a summer night with croaking frogs
In an ancient village,
While the falling stars are flying, who would

Tie a knot for you with the black silk from her hair,
And say she wishes to string the pearls that light up a ship's
channel
As a gift of perpetual friendship?

Thinking of certain distant dates,
Certain distant footsteps on the sand . . .

Tears fall in the night,
Like dying stars that drop
To the bottom of an ancient pool in the woods.

CH'EN MENG-CHIA (b. 1911)

Hesitation

In darkness you held my hand,
You hesitated, nor did I move.
I said nothing, as words remained in my throat,
And a breeze made me shiver slightly.

A soft breath issued from our mouth; I felt
It pass through my body and my heart;
I yearned to keep that moment forever,
But it fled without a pause.

TU YÜN-HSIEH (b. 1920?)

Not a Love Poem

The mountains grow somber, and trees crowd together;
The flowers and herbs lose their colors.
My dear, more than ever are your eyes black
And gleaming, quickening my pulsation.
Please, won't you move your lips again;
I long for more dizziness: We have,
In the gyration of the earth,
Carried with us many a brilliant galaxy.

For give me for again and again giving myself an order
And canceling the order, and again and again cursing
The shouting of the policemen on guard in the city
That threatens and complains in turns.
Now, my dear, let us only soar afar,
Let us melt, let us atone
For those impatient and unlucky tears
And that shameful bit of jealousy.

Let us be like those two blossoms of light white clouds
That fly farther and grow lighter, finally to disappear
In the calm blue. Man can never again
Gossip about their romance
As untamably wild. We shall
Lean together, reminiscing of our happiness while
beautiful dreams
Circulate through the silent contact;
We'll watch how the haze of the evening is quietly
carried away.

WEN CHIEH

from *Love Song of Turfan*

Young lad under the apple tree,
Please don't, don't sing any more;
A girl is coming along the creek,
Her young heart throbs in her bosom.
Why is her heart throbbing so,
So violently, even skipping beats?

Springtime, she works in the orchard,
The songs pass by her ears softly,
The buds on the boughs are not yet open,
The young lad already hopes for fruit.
She cannot understand his strange ideas,
She says, "Don't bother me with your songs."

The young man spends the summer in the orchard,
Gazing at her all the time while working.
The fruits are only as big as grapes,
In his songs he already urges their picking.
She cannot guess all his thoughts,
She days, "Don't stick to me like a shadow."

Pink fruits weigh low the green branches,
Autumn is a season of ripening,
Night after night she cannot sleep.
Is she thinking of the tree full of good apples?
These things he should understand, she says,
"There is something, why don't you say it?"

. . . Young lad under the apple tree,
Please don't, don't sing any more:
She is coming, treading on the meadow,
What is she hiding behind her smiles?
Say it out, what lies truly in your heart.
It's time to harvest the love sown long ago.

Czech Love Poems

FRANTIŠEK GELLNER (1881–1914)

Elegy

The scent of your breath was
like the juice of southern mulberries;
your hair gave off a glare of meadow's air
around your head.
Your dusky eyes were shining like opals
in the evening light,
and your lips were glowing
like red poppies in full bloom.

From the book of my life, woman,
I tore page after page,
and where one might have read your name
all has been already burned.

But who has ever known one's own heart?
In a frame of brass,
our image
follows me throughout the world.

You were not the kind to be forgotten
for another.
Today I know: No other in this world.
Not even you.

FRANTIŠEK HALAS (1901–1949)

Confession

Touched by all that love is
I draw closer toward you
Saddened by all that love is
I run from you

Surprised by all that love is
I remain alert in stillness
Hurt by all that love is
I yearn for tenderness

Defeated by all that love is
at the truthful mouth of the night
Forsaken by all that love is
I will grow toward you.

JAN ALDA (1901–1970)

Going to You

I love the darkness of your gate,
  the evening, when it draws its curtains.
I hear your voice calling me.
  I go as if I am on a horse.

I will put on a festive coat,
  in my lapel a flower,
Although I am not Jesus Christ,
  in front of me the darkness will part.

In your garden the vine sprawls out.
  My hands are very much alike,
when your golden hair
  the fingertips untwine.

BOHUMIL HRABAL (1914–1997)

Morning Gift

You walk
in the fragrance of the departing dusk
on slices of cork.
At times
the pea-pod of your lips bursts
and white peas spill out
in pairs.
At such moments I wish
to inscribe into the snow white of your smile
a few colorful words,
assuming
that in the morning you will
read it all in the mirror
while you hold
in your left hand
a nylon tooth-brush.

Sleeping Nude

I like so much to look at you,
when dressed in a handful of daisies
you reflect the evening sky.
I like so much to look at you,
when from underneath your lashes
the stars fall down onto your blue breast,
and it starts to turn blush
because the moon is setting slowly
and the sun has not yet risen.

EVA BERNARDINOVÁ (b. 1931)

Golden Fish

The moon used to go behind a ship
used to go
the moon and the boat were ploughing the sea
small fish used to glitter in the furrow

And once a beautiful prince came
and didn't need even a fishing net

He was beautiful
as if I were that golden fish

A fish is a submerged bird
and dust
is the time through which hours flow.

IVA HERCÍKOVÁ (1935)

Sadness

I yearn for you
lustfully, in dizziness
wishing that you would come

I think of you
gently, with a smile
wishing to give you joy

I miss you with sadness
only a little bit
wishing not to frighten you

English Love Poems

GEOFFREY CHAUCER (?1343–1400)

Balade

Hide, Absalom, thy gilté tresses clear;
Esther, lay thou thy meekness all a-down;
Hide, Jonathan, all thy friendly mannér;
Penelope and Marcia Catóun
Make of your wifehood no comparisón;
Hide ye your beauties, Isolde and Elaine:
My lady com'th, that all this may distain.

Thy fairé body let it not appear,
Lavine; and thou, Lucrece of Romé town,
And Polixene, that boughten love so dear,
And Cleopatre, with all thy passión,
Hide ye your truth of love and your renown;
And thou, Thisbe, that hast for love such pain:
My lady com'th, that all this may distain.

Hero, Dido, Laodámia, all y-fere,
And Phyllis, hanging for they Demophon,
And Cánacé, espièd by thy chere,
Hypsípylé, betraysèd with Jasón,
Make of your truthé neither boast ne soun;
Nor Hypermestre or Ariadne, ye twain:
My lady com'th, that all this may distain.

SIR PHILIP SIDNEY (1554–1586)

The Bargain

My true love hath my heart, and I have his,
By just exchange, one for the other given.
I hold his dear, and mine he cannot miss,
There never was a better bargain driven.
His heart in me keeps me and him in one,
My heart in him his thoughts and senses guides;
He loves my heart, for once it was his own,
I cherish his, because in me it bides.
His heart his wound receivèd from my sight,
My heart was wounded with his wounded heart;
For as from me on him his hurt did light,
So still methought in me his hurt did smart.
Both equal hurt, in this change sought or bliss:
My true love hath my heart and I have his.

JOHN LYLY (?1554–1606)

Cards and Kisses

Cupid and my Campaspe played
At cards for kisses, Cupid paid;
He stakes his quiver, bow, and arrows,
His mother's doves, and team of sparrows;
Loses them too; then, down he throws
The coral of his lip, the rose
Growing on's cheek (but none knows how);
With these, the crystal of his brow,
And then the dimple of his chin:
All these did my Campaspe win.
At last, he set her both his eyes;
She won, and Cupid blind did rise.
    O Love! has she done this to thee?
    What shall (alas!) become of me?

WILLIAM SHAKESPEARE (1564–1616)

At the Moated Grange

Take, O! take those lips away,
That so sweetly were forsworn,
And those eyes, the break of day,
Lights that do mislead the morn;
But my kisses bring again,
Bring again,
Seals of love, but sealed in vain,
Sealed in vain.

Sonnets

(i)

Shall I compare thee to a summer' day?
Though art more lovely and more temperate:
Rough winds do shake the darling buds of May,
And summer's lease hath all too short a date:
Sometime too hot the eye of heaven shines,
And often is his gold complexion dimmed;
And every fair from fair sometime declines,
By chance, or nature's changing course untrimmed;
But thy eternal summer shall not fade,
Nor lose possession of that fair thou owest,
Nor shall death brag thou wanderest in his shade,
When in eternal lines to time thou growest;
So long as men can breathe, or eyes can see,
So long lives this, and this gives life to thee.

JOHN DONNE (1573–1631)

The Good-morrow

I wonder by my troth, what thou, and I
Did, till we lov'd? were we not wean'd till then?
But suck'd on countrey pleasures, childishly?
Or snorted we in the seven sleepers den?
T'was so; But this, all pleasures fancise bee.
If ever any beauty I did see,
Which I desir'd, and got, t'was but a dreame of thee.

And now good morrow to our waking soules,
Which watch not one another out of feare;
For love, all love of other sights controules,
And makes one little roome, and every where.
Let sea-discoveres to new worlds have gone,
Let Maps to others, worlds on worlds have showne,
Let us possesse one world, each hath one, and is one.

My face in thine eye, thine in mine appeares,
And true plaine hearst doe in the faces rest,
Where can we finds two better hemishpeares
Without sharpe North, without declining West?
What ever dies, was not mixt equally;
If our two loves be one, or, thou and I
Love so alike, that none doe slacken, none can die.

BEN JONSON (?1573–1637)

To Celia

Drink to me only with thine eyes,
And I will pledge with mine;
Or leave a kiss but in the cup
And I'll not look for wine.
The thirst that from the soul doth rise
Doth ask a drink divine;
But might I of Jove's nectar sup,
I would not change for thine.

I sent thee late a rosy wreath,
Not so much honouring thee
As giving it a hope that there
It could not withered be;
But thou theron didst only breathe,
And sent'st it back to me;
Since when it grows, and smells, I swear,
Not of itself but thee!

ROBERT HERRICK (1591–1674)

To the Virgins, to Make Much of Time

Gather ye rosebuds while ye may,
  Old Time is still a-flying:
And this same flower that smiles to-day
  To-morrow will be dying.

The glorious lamp of heaven, the sun,
  The higher he's a-getting,
The sooner will his race be run,
  And nearer he's to setting.

That age is best which is the first,
  When youth and blood are warmer;
But being spent, the worse, and worst
  Times still succeed the former.

Then be not coy, but use your time,
  And while ye may, go marry:
For having lost but once your prime,
  You may for ever tarry.

EDMUND WALLER (1606–1687)

On a Girdle

That which her slender waist confined
Shall now my joyful temples bind;
No monarch but would give his crown
His arms might do what this has done.

It was my Heaven's extremest sphere,
The pale which held that lovely deer:
My joy, my grief, my hope, my love,
Did all within this circle move.

A narrow compass! and yet there
Dwelt all that's good, and all that's fair!
Give me but what this ribband bound,
Take all the rest the sun goes round!

ANDREW MARVELL (1621–1678)

To His Coy Mistress

Had we but world enough, and time,
This coyness, Lady, were no crime.
We would sit down and think which way
To walk and pass our long love's day.
Thou by the Indian Ganges' side
Shouldst rubies find: I by the tide
Of Humber would complain. I would

Love you ten years before the Flood,
And you should, if you please, refuse
Till the conversion of the Jews.
My vegetable love should grow
Vaster than empires, and more slow;
An hundred years should go to praise
Thine eyes and on thy forehead gaze;
Two hundred to adore each breast;
But thirty thousand to the rest;
An age at least to every part,
And the last age should show your heart;
For, Lady, you deserve this state,
Nor would I love at lower rate.
   But at my back I always hear
Time's winged chariot hurrying near;
And yonder all before us lie
Deserts of vast eternity.
Thy beauty shall no more be found,
Nor, in thy marble vault, shall sound
My echoing song: then worms shall try
That long preserved virginity,
And your quaint honour turn to dust,
And into ashes all my lust:
The grave's a fine and private place,
But none, I think, do there embrace,
   Now therefore, while the youthful hue
Sits on thy skin like morning dew,
And while thy willing soul transpires
At every pore with instant fires,
Now let us sport us while we may,
And now, like amorous birds of prey,
Rather at once our time devour
Than languish in his slow-chapt power.
Let us roll all our strength and all
Our sweetness up into one ball,
And tear our pleasures with rough strife
Through the iron gates of life:
Thus, though we cannot make our sun
Stand still, yet we will make him run.

JOHN DRYDEN (1631–1700)

Farewell, Ungrateful Traitor

Farewell, ungrateful traitor,
Farewell, my perjured swain,
Let never injured creature
Believe a man again.
The pleasure of possessing
Surpasses all expressing,
But 'tis too short a blessing,
And love too long a pain.

'Tis easy to deceive us
In pity of your pain,
But when we love you leave us
To rail at you in vain.
Before we have descried it
There is no bliss beside it,
But she that once has tried it
Will never love again.

The passion you pretended
Was only to obtain,
But when the charm is ended
The charmer you disdain.
Your love by ours we measure
Till we have lost our treasure,
But dying is a pleasure,
When living is a pain.

ALEXANDER POPE (1688–1744)

Chloe

'Yet Chloe sure was formed without a spot' —
Nature in her then erred not, but forgot.
'With every pleasing, every prudent part,
Say, what can Chloe want?' — She wants a heart.
She speaks, behaves, and acts just as she ought;
But never, never, reached one generous thought.
Virtue she finds too painful an endeavour,
Content to dwell in decencies forever.
So very reasonable, so unmoved,
As never yet to love, or to be loved.
She, while her lover pants upon her breast,
Can mark the figures on an Indian chest;
And when she sees her friend in deep despair,
Observes how much a chintz exceeds mohair.
Forbid it Heaven, a favour or a debt
She e'er should cancel — but she may forget.
Safe is your secret still in Chloe's ear;
But none of Chloe's shall you ever hear.
Of all her Dears she never slandered one,
But cares not if a thousand are undone.
Would Chloe know if you're alive or dead?
She bids her foootman put it in her head.
Chloe is prudent — would you to be wise?
Then never break your heart when Chloe dies.

WILLIAM BLAKE (1757–1827)

The Clod and the Pebble

'Love seeketh not itself to please,
Nor for itself hath any care,
But for another gives it ease,
And builds a Heaven in Hell's despair.'

So sung a little Clod of Clay
Trodden with the cattle's feet,
But a Pebble of the brook
Warbled out these metres meet:

'Love seeketh only self to please,
To bind another to its delight,
Joys in another's loss of ease,
And builds a Hell in Heaven's despite.'

WILLIAM WORDSWORTH (1770–1850)

A Complaint

There is a change — and I am poor;
Your love hath been, not long ago,
A fountain at my fond heart's door,
Whose only business was to flow;
And flow it did; not taking heed
Of its own bounty, or my need.

What happy moments did I count!
Blest was I then all bliss above!
Now, for that consecrated fount
Of murmuring, sparkling, living love,
What have I? shall I dare to tell?
A comfortless and hidden well.

A well of love — it may be deep —
I trust it is, — and never dry:
What matter? if the waters sleep
In silence and obscurity.
— Such change, and at the very door
Of my fond heart, hath made me poor.

WALTER SAVAGE LANDOR (1775–1864)

Rose Aylmer

Ah, what avails the sceptred race!
   Ah, what the form divine!
What every virtue, every grace!
   Rose Aylmer, all were thine.

Rose Aylmer, whom these wakeful eyes
   May weep, but never see,
A night of memories and sighs
   I consecrate to thee.

JAMES LEIGH HUNT (1784–1859)

Jenny Kissed Me

Jenny kissed me when we met,
   Jumping from the chair she sat in;
Time, you thief, who love to get
   Sweets into your list, put that in!
Say I'm weary, say I'm sad,
   Say that health and wealth have missed me,
Say I'm growing old, but add,
   Jenny kissed me.

GEORGE GORDON NOEL, LORD BYRON (1788–1824)

She walks in beauty, like the night

Of cloudless climes and starry skies;
And all that's best of dark and bright
Meet in her aspect and her eyes:
Thus mellowed to that tender light
Which heaven to gaudy day denies.

One shade the more, one ray the less,
Had half impaired the nameless grace
Which waves in every raven trees,
Or softly lightens o'er her face;
Where thoughts serenely sweet express
How pure, how dear their dwelling-place.

And so that cheek, and o'er that brow,
So soft, so calm, yet eloquent,
The smiles that win, the tints that glow,
But tell of days in gooodness spent,
A mind at peace with all below,
A heart whose love is innocent.

PERCY BYSSHE SHELLEY (1792–1822)

Song

A window bird sate mourning for her love
  Upon a wintry bough;
The frozen wind crept on above,
  The freezing stream below.

There was no leaf upon the forest bare,
  No flower upon the ground,
And little motion in the air
  Except the mill-wheel's sound.

JOHN KEATS (1795–1821)

To Fanny Brawne

This living hand, now warm and capable
Or earnest grasping, would, if it were cold
And in the icy silence of the tomb,
So haunt thy days and chill thy dreaming nights
That thou wouldst wish thine own heart dry of blood
So in my veins red life might stream again,
And thou be conscience-calmed — see here it is —
I hold it towards you.

ELIZABETH BARRETT BROWNING (1806–1861)

Sonnets from the Portuguese

(i)

I thought once how Theocritus had sung
Of the sweet years, the dear and wished-for years,
Who each one in a gracious hand appears
To bear a gift for mortals, old or young:
And, as I mused it in his antique tongue,
I saw, in gradual vision through my tears,
The sweet, sad years, the melancholy years,
Those of my own life, who by turns had flung
A shadow across me. Straightway I was 'ware,
So weeping, how a mystic Shape did move
Behind me, and drew me backward by the hair;
And a voice said in mastery, while I strove, —
'Guess now who holds thee?' — 'Death,' I said. But, there,
The silver answer rang, — 'Not Death, but Love.'

(ii)

If thou must love me, let it be for naught
Except for love's sake only. Do not say,
'I love her for her smile — her look — her way
Of speaking gently, — for a trick of thought
That falls in well with mine, and certes brought
A sense of pleasant ease on such a day' —
For these things in themselves, Beloved, may
Be changed, or change for thee — and love, so wrought,
May be unwrought so. Neither love me for
Thine own dear pity's wiping my cheeks dry:
A creature might forget to weep, who bore
Thy comfort long, and lose thy love thereby!
But love me for love's sake, that evermore
Thou mayst love on, through love's eternity.

(iii)

When our two souls stand up erect and strong,
   Face to face, silent, drawing nigh and nigher,
   Until the lengthening wings break into fire
At either curved point, — what bitter wrong
Can the earth do to us, that we should not long
   Be here contented? Think! In mounting higher,
   The angels would press on us, and aspire
To drop some golden orb of perfect song
Into our deep, dear silence. Let us stay
   Rather on earth, Beloved — where the unfit
Contrarious moods of men recoil away
   And isolate pure spirits, and permit
A place to stand and love in for a day,
   With darkness and the death-hour rounding it.

ALFRED, LORD TENNYSON (1809–1892)

Now Sleeps the Crimson Petal

Now sleeps the crimson petal, now the white;
Nor waves the cypress in the palace walk;
Nor winks the gold fin in the porphyry font:
The fire-fly wakens: waken thou with me.

Now droops the milkwhite peacock like a ghost,
And like a ghost she glimmers on to me.

Now lies the Earth all Danaë to the stars,
And all thy heart lies open unto me.

Now slides the silent meteor on, and leaves
A shining furrow, as thy thoughts in me.

Now folds the lily all her sweetness up,
And slips into the bosom of the lake:
So fold thyself, my dearest, thou, and slip
Into my bosom and be lost in me.

ROBERT BROWNING (1812–1889)

Love in a Life

Room after room,
I hunt the house through
We inhabit together.
Heart, fear nothing, for, heart, thou shalt find her —
Next time, herself! — not the trouble behind her
Left in the curtain, the couch's perfume!
As she brushed it, the cornice-wreath blossomed anew:
Yon looking-glass gleamed at the wave of her feather.

Yet the day wears,
And door succeeds door;
I try the fresh fortune —
Range the wide house from the wing to the centre.
Still the same chance! she goes out as I enter.
Spend my whole day in the quest, — who cares?
But 'tis twilight, you see, — with such suites to explore,
Such closets to search, such alcoves to importune!

MATTHEW ARNOLD (1822–1888)

Dover Beach

The sea is calm to-night.
The tide is full, the moon lies fair
Upon the straits; — on the French coast the light
Gleams and is gone; the cliffs of England stand,
Glimmering and vast, out in the tranquil bay.
Come to the window, sweet is the night-air!
Only, from the long line of spray
Where the sea meets the moon-blanched land,
Listen! you hear the grating roar
Of pebbles which the waves draw back, and fling,
At their return, up the high strand,
Begin, and cease, and then again begin,
With tremulous cadence slow, and bring
The eternal note of sadness in.

Sophocles long ago
Heard it on the Ægæan, and it brought
Into his mind the turbid ebb and flow
Of human misery; we
Find also in the sound a thought,
Hearing it by this distant northern sea.

The Sea of Faith
Was once, too, at the full, and round earth's shore
Lay like the folds of a bright girdle furled.
But now I only hear
Its melancholy, long, withdrawing roar,
Retreating, to the breath
Of the night-wind, down the vast edges drear
And naked shingles of the world.

Ah, love, let us be true
To one another! for the world, which seems
To lie before us like a land of dreams,
So various, so beautiful, so new,
Hath really neither joy, nor love, not light,
Nor certitude, nor peace, nor help for pain;
And we are here as on a darkling plain
Swept with confused alarms of struggle and flight,
Where ignorant armies clash by night.

CHRISTINA GEORGINA ROSSETTI (1830–1894)

A Birthday

My heart is like a singing bird
    Whose nest is in a watered shoot;
My heart is like an apple-tree
    Whose boughs are bent with thickset fruit;
My heart is like a rainbow shell
    That paddles in a halcyon sea;
My heart is gladder than all these
    Because my love is come to me.

Raise me a dais of silk and down;
    Hang it with vair and purple dyes;
Carve it in doves and pomegranates,
    And peacocks with a hundred eyes,
Work it in gold and silver grapes,
    In leaves and silver fleurs-de-lys;
Because the birthday of my life
    Is come, my love is come to me.

THOMAS HARDY (1840–1928)

On the Departure Platform

We kissed at the barrier; and passing through
She left me, and moment by moment got
Smaller and smaller, until to my view
   She was but a spot;

A wee white spot of muslin fluff
That down the diminishing platform bore
Through hustling crowds of gentle and rough
   To the carriage door.

Under the lamplight's fitful glowers,
Behind dark groups from far and near,
Whose interests were apart from ours,
   She would disappear;

Then show again, till I ceased to see
That flexible form, that nebulous white;
And she who was more than my life to me
   Had vanished quite.

We have penned new plans since that fair fond day,
And in season she will appear again —
Perhaps in the same soft white array —
   But never as then!

— 'And why, young man, must eternally fly
A joy you'll repeat, if you love her well?
— O friend, nought happens twice thus; why,
   I cannot tell!

GERARD MANLEY HOPKINS (1844–1889)

Pied Beauty

Glory be to God for dappled things —
For skies of couple-colour as a brinded cow;
For rose-moles all in stipple upon trout that swim;
Fresh-firecoal chestnut-falls; finches' wings;
Landscape plotted and pieced — fold, fallow, and plough;
And áll trádes, their gear and tackle and trim.

All things counter, original, spare, strange;
Whatever is fickle, freckled (who knows how?)
With swift, slow; sweet, sour; adazzle, dim;
He fathers-forth whose beauty is past change:
Praise him.

Finnish Love Poems

Missing Him

Should my treasure come
my darling step by
I'd know him by his coming
recognize him by his step
though he were still a mile off
or two miles away.
As mist I'd go out
as smoke I would reach the yard
as sparks I would speed
as flame I would fly;
I'd bowl along beside him
pout before his face.

I would touch his hand
though a snake were in his palm
I would kiss his mouth
though doom stared him in the face
I'd climb on his neck
though death were on his neck bones
I'd stretch beside him
though his side were all bloody.
And yet my treasure has not
his mouth bloody from a wolf
his hands greasy from a snake
nor his neck in death's clutches:
his mouth if of melted fat
his lips are as of honey
his hands golden, fair
his neck like a heather stalk.

Hopeless Love

From my heart I love you for life,
though my hope is all for naught.

You weren't really going to leave me like this;
it was for my poverty I was abandoned.

You gave me your heart yet took it back again,
for another, you weaned me off your love.

I wish I could write down all the love
that now hurts and burns my heart —

The spark of love you kindled in my breast
unlikely will fade 'fore I go to my grave.

As the sun shines ablaze in the sky,
so beautiful too was our budding love.

TOIVO LYY (1898–1976)

Quietly my wife
breaths beside me,
her dear, beautiful head
across my heart.

Sometimes the heart may carry
a burden kind and gentle.

KATRI VALA (1901–1944)

The memories of all the passionate embraces
are lost behind the days.

But once
you quietly kissed my forehead
as you left me
in the gentle snowfall.
And all around was white tenderness
So lovely, so tearful.

The memory of that moment
unfolds during blue nights
like a quiet flower
replete with fragile fragrance,
and my heart is filled
only with trembling goodness.

YRJÖ JYLHÄ (1903–1956)

Shadows

As the moon shines
I am jealous of my own shadow.
As my shadow melts together with your
    shadow on the snow
I watch it dejectedly.

I may kiss your thirsty lips
and your burning skin,
your splendid, fragrant body
I may conquer hundredfold —

yet for me that is not enough!
I want to tear you open,
I want to merge with you
as our two shadows merge.

EEVA KILPI (b. 1928)

Tell me right away if I'm disturbing you,
he said as he stepped inside my door,
and I'll leave at once.

You not only disturb me, I said,
you shatter my entire existence.
Welcome.

In the morning I write,
in the afternoon I make poetry,
at night I look down the road, drink wine and dance.
What a solo dancer the world has lost in me.

The one who doesn't come
will never know what he's missing.

Song of Love

And one day
we bend forward and reach around each other
and with a click get linked together never again to come loose,
your ailing limbs interlocked with my gout,
my stomach ulcer beside your heart condition
and my arthritis against your sciatica,
we will never, ever part.

And, my dear, you forget your arhythmia, your shortness of breath
and the gangrene
which already resides in your heart
and I forget my catarrh, my restless legs
and the nagging pain in my left side
and may frost and troubles and sorrow come too.

Take my breasts, empty and flat
into your hands, my dear,
for one day as you look at them they will hang low,
will you love me then
My bumble bee, my humble-bumble boy?

Lord, teach us to accept the love of the aged,
the love of the young, the love of the middle-aged,
and the love of the ugly, the love of the poor,
the love of the ragged
and the love of the lonely.
Teach us to accept love,
for we fear it so.

And you take my breasts into your hands,
my drooping flat breasts,
and you caress my crumpled nipples with your lips
and with cataract in your eyes and in queue for a sickbed
blindly you grope for me,
you feel me out with your hands.

Just feel away:
under all these wrinkles it is me,
life has in the end forced upon us this disguise,
    my honeyberry, my dove, my very own swallow.
And my bumps settle into your hollows,
your wrinkles into my grooves
and at your sufferings' bedside I quietly pray for your death.
    Bright is the day and the evening.

PERTTI NIEMINEN (b. 1929)

Al has been said already, written:
I'm just saying it to you, to you
    once more.

At last I got to touch you.
Lucky fingers,
    remained in sweet remembrance
    in the scent of our skin.

I never remember your face,
I remember with my skin

Your breasts, your hip,
your eyes
    in the midst of this world, of this

How wordy
    this love of mine
not a stalk of grass in warm rain,
    not a flower:
as aspen awakened by a midday breeze.

If only I really were a tree, a stalk of grass.
And you another: like in the ballad
we'd tie our crowns, our blossoms, together,
we'd let the wind whistle.
Or you a bird, I a tree,
you not even a little bird:
        I'd hide you anyway. People would say:
listen, the tree sings,
        they'd marvel.

You are a willow warbler
I a willow tree,
        you flutter into my arms each night,
you fall asleep under my arms each night,
you fall asleep under my arm, splutter your
    dreams into the wind
        only for me to hear,
for me, for me too to dream,
you a bird, I a willow.

When I tell you:
I no longer lust for you,
when you are my rest, my peace
so that I may forget you beside me
        only because you are there:
then you can say:
now we are one,
        nothing is between us.
I would not want to die,
for your sake.

PENTTI SAARIKOSKI (1937–1983)

I Love You

I love you
like a foreign country
cliffs and a bridge
like a lonely evening smelling of books
travel the world towards you
under the aerosphere
between two lights
my thought I've carved and you.

MATTIJUHANI KOPONEN (b. 1941)

Under your nightgown
I'd like to be near
the breathing of your skin, listen
to the cells' struggle in life
and death.

And ponder the meaning of it all.
Now that I am already pondering.

Under your nightgown
I'd like to sleep awake
with my eyes open
and listen to the moon breathing
on your skin.

TOMMY TABERMANN (b. 1947)

Go to the forest
Go to the mountain
Go far off to sea
Let loneliness
caress you
until your skin is thin enough
So thin that your heart
sees me through it
that I was the one
who caressed you,
who caresses you
Go, go.

ARJA TIAINEN (b. 1947)

Love has
nothing to do
with opinions, looks, accomplishments.
What love wants from you is
what is underneath.
Spinal cord, bone marrow, skin, scent,
undress, therefore,
layer by layer the entire soul.

Love Poems from Finnish-Swedish Sources

J. L. RUNEBERG (1804–1877)

The Only Moment

Alone was I,
he came alone;
his path led by
the path of mine,
he didn't dwell,
but thought of dwelling,
he didn't speak, his eyes spoke for him —
O total stranger,
yet so familiar!
A day goes by,
a year too passes,
one memory haunts the other;
that fleeting moment,
stayed ever with me,
the bitter moment,
the tender moment.

Three teachings the mother gave her daughter:
Not to sigh, not to be unhappy,
and never to kiss a boy —

Mother, if your daughter does submit,
does submit to your last advice
she shall surely disobey the first two.

The boy reached the age of fifteen — and did not yet think
that there is love in the world;
he lived another five years — and still did not think
that there is love in the world.
Then, without forewarning there came a girl of statuesque
beauty,
who taught him in a few short hours
what for twenty years he'd failed to grasp.

EDITH SÖDERGRAN (1892–1923)

Love

My soul was a light blue dress,
color of the sky;
I left it on a rock on the shore of the sea
and, naked, I came to you resembling a woman.
And as a woman I sat at your table
and drank a glass of wine and inhaled the fragrance of roses.
You found me beautiful
and I reminded you of something you had seen in a dream.
I forgot everything, I forgot my childhood and
my homeland.
I knew only that I was held captive by your sweet caress.
And with a smile you took a mirror and beckoned me look at
myself.
I saw that my shoulders were made of dust and fell to dust,
I saw that my beauty was sick and had only one wish —
to dissolve.
O, hold me in your arms tightly, so that I shall want nothing

French Love Poems

LOUISE LABÉ (1525–1565)

Sonnet 8

I live, I die. I drown and I burn.
I shiver with cold and perish with heat.
I leap from anguish to delight; from sweet
To bitter. No two moments are the same.

Suddenly my laughter and my cries
Join in a single instant, each pleasure
Aches with a hidden torment, and the night
Fades, yet endures. I wither and I bloom.

So Love leads me on forever.
And when I think I know the limits of pain
Without knowing, I find myself at peace.

When I think my joy is lasting and I see
Some future hope, some present certainty,
He returns and brings back the past again.

VICTOR HUGO (1802–1885)

The Vase

Since I have often placed my lips to your overflowing cup,
Since in your soft hands I have often placed my pale brow,
Since I have often breathed the heavenly sweet fragrance,
Of your soul, enshrined in the darkness of shadows;

Since it was given to me to hear the secret mysteries
That dwell within the most sacred recess of your heart,
Since I have seen you cry and I have seen you smile,
Your lips upon my lips, your eyes upon my eyes;

Since from your veiled star I have often seen the rays
Shining on my ravished brow and holding me a slave,
Since I have seen full on the water of my life
A rose petal plucked from your sweet days,

I now defy the years in their impetuous flight:
Pass on! pass on! I no longer grow old!
Flee on with all your garland flowers that die,
I have within my soul a flower you cannot pluck.

Your wings may smite it but never sill a drop
From my abundant vase as it slakes my thirst,
Your ashes can never smother my soul's flame
And oblivion can never quench my eternal love.

STÉPHANE MALLARMÉ (1842–1898)

Apparition

The moon was languishing. Seraphim dreaming in tears,
With bows in their hands in the calm of the vaporous
Flowers, free from the dying violins
White sobs gliding the azure of the corollas.
— It was the blessed day of your first kiss.
My dreaming, delighted in my martyrdom,
Became drunk with the perfume of sadness
Which the gathering of a Dream, without regret
Or disenchantment, leaves within the heart.
And so I wandered, with my eye fixed on the aged road
When with the sunlight in your hair, on the street
And in the evening, laughing you appeared to me
And I thought I saw a fairy with a radiant hat
Who in former times would pass over my slumbers
Of a spoiled child, always spreading form her loose hands
Snow white bouquets of perfumed stars.

PAUL VERLAINE (1844–1896)

Sentimental Colloquy

In the ancient park, solitary and vast,
Two forms only moments ago just passed.

Their lips barely move and their eyes are dead,
And one scarcely heard the words they said.

In the deserted old park now frozen fast,
Two specters summoned up their past.

— Do you remember our old ecstasy?
— Why would you bring it back again to me?

— Does your heart still throb hearing my name so?
Does my soul still appear in your reveries? — No.

— Ah, the old days, what joys have they seen
When your lips met my lips! It may have been.

— How blue was the sky, and our hope, how light!
— Hope has been vanquished back into the night.

In the weeds and dead grasses their steps led,
And only the night heard the words they said.

LÉON-PAUL FARGUE (1876–1947)

Words

The words, the special words she had for me,
I listened as she said them to another.
I hear the sabre sound on the wood of the bed.
I will hear all of her words.
When he kisses her on the eyes, there at the
edge of the island where a lamp is burning, he
feels her eyelids beating beneath his mouth like
the head of a bird which has been captured
and is scared . . .

He slowly moves along the network of veins as
the faint shadow of an underwater plant . . .
With his whole body he caresses the breasts
made poisonous by love . . .

I will hear everything in the corridor with thin
partitions, all white with windows, with this vapid,
sweet smell of wood scorched by the sun . . .

Sometimes I waited for a long time before her
door and in a place so well known that it made
me sick. I knocked. I heard the empty space
sprawling behind . . . Next door they were walking
quickly as if to come and open . . .

Somewhere a clock was mourning. Evening fell
through the glazed bays on the steps . . .

Then the surge of the autumn wind, the murmuring
of the trees on the ramparts, the smell of rain in the
moats, and many songs of Paris passed over her . . .

PAUL ELUARD (1895–1952)

The Curve of Your Eyes

The curve of your eyes circles my heart,
A round of dance and gentleness,
Time's aureole, safe nocturnal cradle,
And if I don't remember all that I have lived
Blame your eyes that haven't always seen me.

Leaves of day and moss of dew,
Reeds of the wind, perfumed smiles,
Wings spreading light over the world,
Boats laden with the sky and the sea,
Hunters of noises and springs of colors

Perfumes bursting from a myriad dawns
Always lying on a pallet of stars,
As the day depends on innocence
the whole world depends upon your clear eyes
And all my blood flows within their gaze.

JACQUES PRÉVERT (1900–1977)

For You My Love

I went to the market of birds
And I bought some birds
For you
my love

I went to the market of flowers
And I bought some flowers
For you
my love

I went to the market of iron
And I bought some chains
Some heavy chains
For you
my love

Then I went to the market of slaves
And I searched for you
But I did not find you there
my love.

ANDRÉ FRÉNAUD (b. 1907)

I Have Never Forgotten You

Now without name, without face,
with nothing more of your eyes or pallor.

Unleashed from my desire's assault
on your misleading image, stripped
by the false confessions of time,
ransomed by the false coins of love,
by all of these gains that have been lost,
freed from you now, free as a dead man,
living an empty life alone,
with the stones and leaves,

When I am between the breasts of
other, gentle unloved women, I still
lie on your absence, on the living corpse
you make through your power ordained
to destroy me to the end of my silence.

German Love Poems

JOHANN WOLFGANG VON GOETHE (1749–1832)

If you wish to enjoy the pure feeling of love's delight,
  Let insolence and gravity both be far from your heart.
The former will drive away Amor, the latter plans to
    enchain him;
  The god in his knavishness smiles at the contrast they offer.

~ ~

Ha! I know you, Love, as well, as another; you bring
  Your torch, and it sheds its light on the shadows before us.
But you take us quickly down the tangled path; we have
    need for
  Your torch more than ever; ah, the faithless thing goes out.

~ ~

Thoughts by Night

You I pity, miserable stars,
that are fair and shine so splendidly,
lend your light to distressed fishermen,
unrewarded both by men and gods;
for you love not, never knew what love is!
But relentlessly eternal hours
lead your legions through the far-flung heavens.
Ah, what journey have you just completed
since I, resting in my loved one's arms,
did not even thing of you at midnight.

Nearness of Her Lover

I think of you when the sun's glorious shimmer
shines from the sea;
I think of you when the moon's pallid glimmer
edges the tree.

I behold you when on the distant ridge
The dust throws veils,
in deepest night when on the narrow bridge
the wanderer quails.

I hear your voice when roaring billows glisten
in thunderous riot.
In the still grove I often walk to listen
when all is quiet.

I am with you, however far you are,
I feel you near.
The sun goes down, soon comes the evening star.
That you were here!

Ah, who brings the happy moments,
Glorious days of sweet first love;
Who can bring back a single hour
Of that blessed time again.

A sight for the Immortals
A happy loving pair,
The best of spring's fair weather
Is not so warm and fair.

FRANZ GRILLPARZER (1791–1872)

A Kiss

A hand is to be kissed with reverence,
The forehead — solemnly, with friendship,
The cheeks — with tender admiration,
And the lips be kissed with ardor,
While the eyes one kisses with langour,
The neck — with passionate desire,
And with a maddening delirium
All the rest is to be kissed.

HEINRICH HEINE (1797–1856)

There was an aged monarch,
His heart was grave, his hair was gray;
This poor old monarch married
A maid that was young and gay.

There was a handsome page-boy,
Blond was his hair, bright was his mien;
He bore the silken train
Of this so youthful queen.

You know this old, old story?
I sounds so sweet, so sad to tell!
The lovers had to perish,
They loved each other too well.

They loved each other, but neither
Would be the first to confess;
Like foes, they gaz'd at each other,
And would die of their love's distress.
from *Buch der Lieder. Die Heimkehr, 36*

FRIEDRICH HEBBEL (1813–1863)

You and I

We dreamed of one another
And wakened to the light;
We live to love each other
And sink back into the night.

You stepped out of my dreaming,
Out of your dream stepped I;
If either is ever wholly
Lost in the other, we die.

Upon a lily tremble
Two clear, round drops. They kiss,
Dissolve into one, and go rolling
Into the throat's abyss.

THEODOR STORM (1817–1888)

Consolation

Let come what will, let come what may!
So long you live, it is still day.

Whenever in the world I roam,
Where'er you are, for me is home.

I gaze upon your lovely face,
No shadows of the future trace.

OTTO JULIUS BIERBAUM (1865–1910)

Come Here and Let Me Kiss You

The air is as if full of violins,
From all the flourishing branches
A white wonder pours down;
Spring rages in the blood,
This is the best time
For all kinds of merriment.

Come here and let me kiss you!
You must submit
To my arm embracing you.
Knocking and shaking
Goes through the whole life:
This is the red blood, it sings, it sings.

HUGO VON HOFMANNSTHAL (1874–1929)

The Two

She bore the goblet in her hand —
her chin and mouth firm as its band —
her stride so weightless and so still
that not a drop would ever spill.

So weightless and so firm his hand:
he rode a young horse for his pleasure
and, looking like incarnate leisure,
compelled it; trembling it must stand.

But when he should take from her hand
the goblet that she lifted up,
the two were quivering so much
that each hand missed the other's touch,
and heavy grew the weightless cup
till dark win rolled upon the sand.

RAINER MARIA RILKE (1875–1926)

Love Song

How could I keep my soul so that it might
not touch on yours? How could I elevate
it over you to reach to other things?
Oh, I would like to hide it out of sight
with something lost in endless darkenings,
in some remote, still place, so desolate
it does not sing whenever your depth sings.
Yet all that touches us, myself and you,
takes us together like a violin bow
that draws a single voice out of two strings.
Upon what instrument have we been strung?
And who is playing with us in his hand?
Sweet is the song.

HANS ARP (1887–1966)

You have smiled
so that you wouldn't cry.
You have smiled
as if bright days
would shine for a long time.
Your wings glittered
like young leaves.
Your face was like a white star.

Since you have died,
I thank every passing day.
Every passing day
brings me closer to you.

MASCHA KALEKO (1912–1975)

Love in the City

Somewhere you meet each other — fleeting —
And sometimes there's a rendezvous.
A something, — it's not worth repeating —
Tempts you to prolong the meeting.
With the second sundae you say "du."

You like each other and anticipate by day
The promise of a night not spent alone.
You'll share the daily worries and dismays,
You'll share the joys of a raise in pay,
. . . The rest is done by telephone.

In the city's tumult you both meet.
Not at home. You live in a room in an apartment.
— Through the confusion, noise, cars on the street,
— Past the gossiping women and girls on the beat,
you go with each other, quiet, confident.

You kiss on a bench along the way,
— Or on a paddle-boat instead.
Eros must be limited to Sundays.
— You think of now — and come what may!
You speak bluntly and do not turn red.

You don't give each other narcissi or roses,
And you don't communicate by servant:
When weekend kisses cease to engross,
Then you send a letter via Federal Post:
"It's over!" written down in shorthand.

Greek Love Poems

The Greek Period

ARCHILOCHOS (8TH CENTURY B.C.)

Love

I live here miserable and broken with desire,
pierced through to the bones by the bitterness
of this god-given painful love.

O comrade, this passion makes my limbs limp
and tramples over me.

SAPPHO (b. 612 B.C.)

To Eros

From all the offspring
of the earth and heaven
love is most precious.

When You Come

You will lie down and
I shall lay out soft
pillows for your body.

Bittersweet Love

[It brings us pain]
and weaves myths.

Eros

Now in my
Heart I
see clearly

A beautiful
face
shining,

etched
by love.

ANAKREON (c. 560 B.C.)

Knockout

Eros, the blacksmith of love,
smashed me with a giant hammer
and doused me in the cold river.

On a Conservative Lover

I love and yet do not love.
I am mad yet not quite mad.

PLATO (c. 427–c. 348 B.C.)

Love Poem

My child — Star — you gaze at the stars,
and I wish I were the firmament
that I might watch you with many eyes.

Sokrates to His Lover

As I kissed Agathon my soul swelled to my lips,
where it hangs, pitiful, hoping to leap across.

The Hellenistic Period

MELEAGROS (c. 140–70 B.C.)

The Wine Cup

The wine cup is happy. It rubbed against
warm Zenophilia's erotic mouth. O bliss!
I wish she would press her lips under my lips
and in one breathless gulp drain down my soul.

The Kiss

Your eyes are fire, Timarian, your kiss birdlime.
You look at me and I burn. You touch me and I stick!

The Roman Period

MARCUS ARGENTARIUS (EARLY CHRISTIAN ERA)

Discreet Witness

As I lay clutching Antigone's body,
my chest throbbed against her bosom,
my lips pressed into her sweet lips —

for the rest you must ask the lamp.

NIKARCHOS (1ST CENTURY A.D.)

Kissing

If you kiss me you hate me; if you hate me
you kiss me,
but if you don't hate me, my sweet friend,
don't kiss me.

Hungarian Love Poems

BÁLINT BALASSI (1554–1594)

When He Chanced upon Julia He Greeted Her Thus

I don't want this world without you, fair love
who stands beside me: good health, my sweetheart!

My woeful heart's cheer, my soul's sweet longing
you are all its joy: God's blessing be yours!

My precious palace, my fragrant red rose
my lovely violet, live long, Julia!

Dawn of my sunlight, your eyebrows' black fire,
my two eyes' bright light: live, live, my life's hope!

My heart burns for you, my soul longs for you:
my heart, soul, love — be blessed, my princess!

Thus Julia I greeted, seeing her:
I bowed knee, bowed head, and she merely smiled.

SÁNDOR KISFALUDY (1772–1844)

The Torments of Love

Song 7
As the stag, when wounded sore
By the cruel hunter's spear,
Flies — too late — for more and more
Gushing veins his flanks besmear,
So I fly form your bright glance,
Seeking to avoid its smart —
All too late, the flying lance
Has already hurt my heart.
And, alas, the more I run,
Worse the festering poison grows;
Thus I feel my heart undone,
Stumbling sink beneath my woes.

Song 90
When I hear sweet music blent
From thy tones of silver fine,
Philomela's rich lament
Never sounded so divine.
Nature listens, mute and lowly,
In a silent ecstasy;
Hearkening rivers run more slowly,
Hush'd the leaves soliloquy.
Hush'd is every bird's high song,
Every Zephyr still'd the while;
Every breeze is lull'd along,
Even pain begins to smile.

MIHÁLY VÖRÖSMARTY (1800–1855)

Revery

For thy love
My brain would pay the toll;
Each thought of it, I bring
To thee on fancy's wing;
I'd give to thee my soul
for they love.

For thy love,
On yonder mountains high,
I'd be a tree, and dare
My head to storm-winds bare;
Each winter willing die
For thy love.

For thy love
I'd be a rock-pressed stone;
Within the earth, its flame
Shall burn my trembling frame;
I'd stand it with no groan
For thy love.

For thy love
My soul I would demand
From God; with virtues I
To deck it out would try
To place them in thy hand
For thy love.

GERGELY CZUCZOR (1800–1866)

The Rain is Falling

The rain is falling on the field;
        In pools it lies.
Wold that one drop would only fall
        From my love's eyes!
After the rain, more radiant flowers
        The meadow bears.
More beautiful my gentle love
        Would grow in tears.
The wind transports the clouds away
        Beyond the north;
Out from behind their gloom the sun
        Comes shining forth.
O that the wind would also take
        My grief away,
And with the presence of my love
        Bring back the day!

MIHÁLY TOMPA (1817–1868)

Burning Love

Whence came the beautiful
Flower of burning love?
Its petals unfolding turn crimson
As if dipped in blood.
Why does it sigh each night
So long, so deep?
When happiness and joy
Its radiant colors seek.
When the wild rose heart
the gleaming petals pierced,
which reddened so from love:
Its precious blood was spilled.
And as it flows and streams,
To the unfaithful one "I was true"
It cries, "you turned away . . .
You murdered me, — I love you!"
And the cold earth drinks its blood,
In it all life cools away . . .
Yet it sends the dead one back
With the smiling spring one day;
For while the heart no longer beats,
Senseless, below the earth it lies,
But what flamed in it before,
That sacred feeling never dies!
Where the wild rose's burning blood
Spilled on the dust of the earth:
The power of its love
Brings a new flower's birth.
Which sighs so long . . . so deep . . .
In the lonely night:
"I remained true, I love you truly
In death, and in life!"

And whose petals turn crimson,
As if dipped in blood:
From spilled blood came
The beautiful flower of burning love.

SÁNDOR VACHOTT (1818–1861)

Folksong

How pretty is the cherry tree
My love's face is fairer to me,
My love blossoms in summer-winter
Fairest of all who are near her.

The clearest blue of her eyes
The cloudlessness of the skies,
The bright star's falling
Her blue eyes' calling.

If her hair of flax were made,
A kings daughter would it braid:
More like satin I do swear
Is each strand of her fine hair.

Till harvest I can hardly wait
For that is our wedding date
Daily I look in the morning light
Did the wheat yellow more overnight?

SÁNDOR PETÕFI (1823–1849)

My Love

A hundred forms my love at times doth take,
And in a hundred shapes appears to me;
Sometimes an isle around which billows break,
The seas — my passions that encircle thee.

And then again, sweet love, thou art a shrine;
So that I think my love luxuriant falls,
Like leafy bowers, verdant and benign,
Around the church's consecrated walls.

Sometimes thou art a traveler, rich and great,
And, like a brigand, on thee breaks my love;
Again it meets thee in a beggar's state
And, suppliant, asks thee for the alms thereof.

Or thou art as the high Carpathian hills,
And I the thunderous cloud that shakes thy heart;
Or thou the rosebush round whose fragrance thrills
The nightingale, whereof I play the part.

Thus my love varies, but doth never cease;
It still remains imperishably sure;
Its strength abides, but with a greater peace;
Oft calm, and yet with depths that will endure.

LAJOS DÓCZI (1845–1919)

What is a Kiss?

Tis understood alone by those who lean
To listen, what a sweet, true kiss doth mean.
Therein there is no right, will, or intent;
Exchanging not, they mutually present —
Born of a minute, as though suddenly
Two sparks should catch and cause a flame to be.
Sweet is the kiss if sleep thy sweetheart sway;
What she might give thou tak'st in stealthy way;
But sweeter still if from the pouting lip
Denying and delaying thou dost sip.
But sweetest 'tis when both a thirst do feel,
And, giving, each from t'other fain would steal.
Yet, if desire exists where no claim lives,
It dares to take, but feels not that it gives;
Indeed, such kisses, which by hundreds thrive,
Not wedded yoke but sweet love keeps alive.
Even this is sweeter when earth's envious eyes,
Like falcon's, watch thee and thy honeyed prize.
The moment comes, thou feelest "now or never!"
Arms fly to arms, lips cling as though forever
Each would be first and each be last in bliss;
Each one is kissed and each doth warmly kiss.
Just as a diver to the depths doth leap,
So doth desire plunge in the moment's deep.
What rapture can a brief span not conceive?
If not forbidden, 'tis no kiss, believe!

JENŐ HELTAI (1871–1957)

Like a Madrigal

How you kissed me and how I kissed you,
How we sat together under the acacia trees
Sometime in May . . . we two . . .
Today it's winter, I don't remember,
How you loved me and how I loved you,
How you embraced me and how I embraced you
Furtively, secretly, obliviously,
Today it's winter, I don't remember.

The winter with its snow covers everything,
Spring has frozen in my heart:
Today it's winter, I don't remember,
How you loved me and how I loved you,
How you embraced me and how I embraced you
How we sat together under the acacia trees,
Sometimes in May . . . we two . . .

ENDRE ADY (1877–1919)

A Half-Kissed Kiss

A half-kissed kiss is wildly before us
Blazing and flaming.
Cold is the evening. Sometimes we hasten,
Weeping we hasten,
Never attaining.

How often we stop. Together we mourn,
Freezing and burning.
Thou thrustest me back. Blood-stained are my lips,
Blood-stained are thy lips,
Yearning and yearning.

This kiss consumed we should peacefully
Die without sorrow.
We long for that kiss, we crave for that fire,
But sadly we say:
Tomorrow, tomorrow.

With Léda at the Ball

The music screams, it towers; perfumed, young
And sultry vapors flutter in the air,
As flower-wreathed young boys and maidens gaze
In terror at the somber couple there.

"Who are these two?" We enter without words,
Our lifeless faces covered by a pall.
We throw our withered roses silently
Among the couples in the joyous hall.

The music dies, and in the merry hall
Wintery breezes blow the flames to sleep.
We start on dancing, as the couples are
Frightened away and shiveringly weep.

Léda in the Garden

In a somber garden yon crimson hammock
Lullingly dangles.
Drooping flowers with tearful petals
Wail for our kisses and wrangles.

I dreamily gaze at you; on the heavens
Purple clouds ramble.
Swaying they trade their fragile kisses
And die in their longings' fire-shamble.

Two purple cloudlets; we fly. Our passions
Flare to be sated;
And here in the garden also the poppies
Pity us satiated.

GYULA JUHÁSZ (1883–19370

I Have Forgot

I have forgot the fairness of her hair;
But this I know, that when the flaming grain
Across the rippling fields makes summer fair,
Within its gold I feel her grace again.

I have forgot the blueness of her eyes;
But when Septembers lay their tired haze
In sweet farewell across the azure skies,
I dream once more the sapphire of her gaze.

I have forgot the softness of her voice;
But when the spring breathes out its softest sigh,
Then I can hear her speak the tender joys
That bless'd the springtime of a day gone by.

MIHÁLY BABITS (1883–1941)

Radiance

How the combs and ringed clips
Come undone and fall asunder:
When you proudly before the mirror
Let lose your sparkling hair!
Your two slim arms stretch
from your shoulders to your tresses,
like an antique pitcher's two handles
that spring forth gracefully.
Oh treasure of pitchers! precious treasure!
Treasure's pitcher! Vessel of kisses!
Nothing is similar to you,
I gaze at you with holy desire!
Living pitcher! of life,
in whom the great elixir stands,
that turns the dead into living
and the beggar into more than a king.
How can I praise your figure?
The palm trees, the cedars,
the mast and the lily —
they do not live, they do not move . . .
But in you each muscle lives,
nerves, muscles and tendons,
secretly like mysterious waves
still billow in the quiet breeze.
Wherever you go, the air
fills with delight, and grows more refined,
and like the halo around a saint
covers your body with an aura of light.
In the stove the flames flare,
on the wall the clock stops,
when you proudly before the mirror
Undo your living waist.

LŐRINC SZABÓ (1900–1957)

Moments

Since yesterday when I kissed you
and you languishing (but just for a moment,
since you protested already) left
my knee between your trembling knees:
constantly gratitude renders you before me,
constantly you stand before me, on the street, at work
constantly I run into you: I see your head
bent back, your burning face,
your closed eyes and tortured beauteous desire's
beautiful smile on your lips.
At such a time I too close my eyes for just
a second and I feel faint:
I feel your nearness, my face bathes in the
sweet lines of your face, your burning breasts
scorch my hand, you kiss me again,
and I awaken terrified: oh, this is but
pure craziness — and still it feels so good
to lose myself in you: your entire body
flows around me and I happily
gallop away in your flaming veins.

Since You Are Nowhere

Since you are nowhere, I look for you all over,
sun, meadow, lake, cloud, a hundred landscapes your cover,
always the world shows you somewhere
and always it hides you, but the mistakes
of my probing eyes lead me to you,
so that light-shadow, fairy zithers
flash your voice, your eyes, your lips,
the silent playfulness of the imagination:
I see you and I don't see you, your dear name
your heart makes resound in my ringing heart,
but from moment to moment I lose you again:
I reach out to the stars and I listen,
your pursuer, I, still, as if pulled down
by lead, into your grave, withdraw into myself.

GYULA ILLYÉS (1902–1983)

To the Wife

From far away, you guard my fate here too.
I lie peacefully. Stronger, tougher,
all the greater, the farther you are.
In the world of your arms I am rocking.

ATTILA JÓZSEF (1905–1937)

That Beautiful Woman From the Past

I would like to see again that beautiful woman from the past,
in whom soft ethereal tenderness enclosed itself,
who when we three took a walk next to the fields,
cheerfully and seriously stepped in the light mud,
who when she glanced at me, made me tremble,
that beautiful woman whom I would love not to love.
I would only like to see her, I have no plans with her,
Sunbathing, daydreaming as she sits there in the garden,
And like herself, a closed book, in her hand
and around her large, thick branches that rustle
in the autumn wind.
I would watch, as she once hesitatingly, slowly
Like one who makes up her mind in the whispery bower,
Stands up and looks around and suddenly departs
And takes to the road, that beyond the garden's shrubs
lies hidden to lead her through the distance
with trees waving farewell on either side;
I would only like to see her, as the child its dead mother
that beautiful woman from the past, as she leaves in the light.

MIKLÓS RADNÓTI (1909–1944)

In Your Arms

In your arms I'm rocking, rocking,
hushaby;
in my arms you're rocking, rocking,
lullaby.
In your arms I am a boychild,
quieting;
in my arms you are a girlchild,
listening.
In your arms you hold me tightly
when I'm scared;
when my arms can hold you tightly
I'm not scared.
When you're holding me, not even
death's huge hushaby
can frighten me.
In your arms through death as dreaming
I will fall so
dreamingly.

SÁNDOR CSOORI (b. 1930)

This Day

One day with you,
one day the madness again:
the dusk of your room and your body,
its quiet and boundlessness.

Your uncovered mouth and nothing else —
outside the sparkle of woodbine:
in the sky a black and blue mark.

It's a daring hope to love like this.
to be born for your breasts, for your mouth,
to blend with the earth and the sky.

Summer, like blood, clots,
like empires, it crumbles:
flowers — ruins,
leaves — the dead
gather 'round us like gentle filth.

Don't be afraid, I'm not, this day
embalms your bed,
your hands, your silence
and I lie beside you even
when sleep carries me home,
when I no longer have words,
only these:
there is wind,
it is evening.

Indian Love Poems

MAST TAVAKKULI (BALUCHI)

Sammo

Sammo is a fig-tree on the hill
Sammo is a blossom on the bough
Sammo is a flagon of good wine
Sammo is a mountain-bred gazelle
Sammo is a pomegranate flower
Sammo is a lamp bright in the dark
Or a plant the rain's helped grow
Sammo is a fig-tree with broad leaves
On a hill or near a lake
Set in deep-sunk mountain glens
Which no wind can ever shake.

The glances from the red-streaked eye
Are lightning darting from the clouds
Her graceful form in silken clothes
Moves like a cloud from far-off lands
Her face is gold, her eyes are fair
Her hair down to her slender waist
Cuts like a sword-blade, fierce and sharp.

CHANDIDAS (BENGALI)

Only a lover will know

Only a lover will know how I feel.

The talk all around me is nothing to me
My heart dwells on no one but him.

I work in the house where I have to keep quiet
My love must remain unrevealed.

Alone in my fear like the wife of a thief
I've no one to comfort my heart.

The senior family members all give
Me curses form morning till night.

I suffer because of the one that I love
Unsupported by anyone here.

Here nobody knows the sharp pain in my heart
To whom can I make my complaint?

So listen to Chandidas: Happiness lies
In letting your love be proclaimed.

ANONYMOUS (Brahui)

Why did she marry another?

Your eyes are magic worth a *lakh* of rupees
Your early teeth are tall as cinnamon trees
Your ram-like eyes are pleasant as a tent
You're mistress of the camp, the home's best flower
The water that you bring is elixir
Go on, my sweet-toothed love, lift up your feet!

My mulberry branch, you have another man
You light up evening, widowed in your youth
The priest proclaims that Souzu is betrothed
Your head's a sunshade, you are all perfume
Your hair-do and jewellery are just like a whore's
First she is betrothed and next she's married
My *pulao*-loving darling, up you go!

Now see how Barag stands upon the road
Now see how Souzu is eaten up with love
You are my dear, my dear, my dearest one
But no, you're shameless, dear to me no more
I'm so unlucky, I'm mocked by everyone
To me she's false, to another she is true!

Keeping the pitcher clean

Cool water flows beneath the moon
I'll drink to you, my beauty
So keep your pitcher clean for me.

In other gardens flowers bloom
Bananas grow in mine
If we're to meet, let's meet tonight
Let's not leave things to future chance.

In other gardens flowers bloom
But cabbages in mine
I will not wheel and deal, my beauty
You are my eyes' one true desire.

No more will I go to the well by myself
I fetch water along with the rest of the girls
No more will I go to the well by myself.

The villagers here are all cruel and unkind
Although they accuse me I have done no wrong
No more will I go to the well by myself.

How can anyone laugh? How can anyone talk?
How can anyone speak to anyone here?
No more will I go to the well by myself.

My mother-in-law and my sister-in-law
Are always suspecting me — what can I do?

No more will I go to the well by myself.

MIRAHAI (GUJARATI)

Rejoicing in the rainy season

The rainy season's clouds now mark
This best time of the year.

My heart flows over with delight
I've heard my Lord will come.

The dark and threatening clouds are here
The lightning brings the rain.

The flashes and the drops of rain
The coolly gentle breeze.

Move Mira, handmaid of the Lord,
To utter songs of joy.

Fill up with water, cloud, and come!

The raindrops fall, the *koil* cries
The breeze blows cool, the thunder rolls.

The sky is filled with heavy clouds
My Love will come today.

I have prepared a bed for Him
So welcome Him with songs.

Says Mira, handmaid of the Lord:
The lucky come to You.

BIHARI LAL (HINDI)

Glimpses

Their glances stretched between the rooftops form
A tightrope for brave lovers' hearts to cross

First making sure none watches them, they stand on tiptoe
Then lean across the wall between for eager kisses

Up to the roof she goes to look, then down
Untiring, like a yo-yo on love's string

Above her yard she sees her lover's kite
And madly runs about to chase its shadow

You praise those pigeons tumbling in the sky
Who is it though who made you look so thrilled?

With arm around him, now she moves, then stops
Flashing like lightning on her balcony

Their hearts so full of love, their talk so full of pain
A million signals sent while walking to the door.

SURDAS (HINDI)

Radha's jealous rage with Krishna

She proudly sits in silence
In trance as if from yogic breath control.

Immobile, eyelids closed, with covered head
But who'll endure the rage she meditates?

'Now go and calm her,' Radha's friend tells Krishna
'Go and you'll see how furious she is.'

'This is no time for anger
The rains are falling, lovers are united.

The heat-burnt creepers clasp the trees afresh
Once dried-up rivers flow down to the sea.

Youth is soon gone, a passing cloud-cast shadow —
I've told you so much else of partnership.

Be sensible and come', says Radha's friend.
'Come then to *your* dear Krishna,' she replies.

THE KAMASUTRA OF VATSYAYANA (1ST CENTURY A.D.)

Kisses Classified

The passion-kindling kiss:
When she looks at this face while he sleeps and kisses it to show her desire.

The distracted kiss:
When she kisses him while he is inattentive or quarrelling or thinking of something else or sleepy.

The awakekning kiss:
When someone comes late at night and to show his desire kisses his beloved who is asleep on the bed.
She may go on seeming to be asleep at the time of her lover's arrival in order to establish his inclinations.

The purposeful kiss:
When someone kisses the reflection of the beloved in a mirror, in water or on a wall.

The transferred kiss:
When someone kisses a child, a picture or a statue.

The challenging kiss:
When a man comes up to a woman at night in the theatre or at a party and kisses on the fingers, or on the toes if she is sitting.
When a woman is massaging her lover and lays her head on his thigh as if overcome by sleep, and to arouse him kisses his thigh or his big toe.

And here there is a verse:

Each act in kind should be repaid
With stroke for stroke, and kiss for kiss

The girls sing back to the boys

The boys:
You two lovely sisters on each side of me
I do so love both of you, but I'm afraid
You'll laugh if I say: 'Wait, get married to me!'
The girls:
O never will we marry, O never at all
Instead we will stay here together at home
As close and as tight as two horns on a ram!

The boys:
O let me feel your breasts
I long to marry you
I cannot pay the price!
The girls:
You cannot feel for free
I'm saving myself for
The man who'll marry me!
The boys:
I love you, don't say no
Who will know if I have
One feel to remember by?
The girls:
I love you too, but first
My parents must be paid
We'll sleep together then!

Getting together

I love your head with waving hair
Tied in a bun with scarlet thread
While you keep weaving wreaths of flowers
I long for you with burning heart.

I love the bangles on your wrist
The shining necklace round your neck
The toe-ring jingles on your feet
I long for you with burning heart.

The couple pass the wineshop, arm in arm
With graceful movement, free from saddening thoughts
Their new-found joy casts out all cares and fears.

With yellow clothes and ornaments of gold
With hearts that beat as one, all gloom is gone
When love unites, farewell to cares and fears.

The more they drink the less they think of who is who
Forgetting everything as heart is joined to heart.

KING SRINIVASA MALLA (NEWARI)

To what shall I compare you?

To what shall I compare your face?
A pool with lotus-blooms for eyes
Your lips made red by betel-juice
Enchant me with each word they speak.

You know how sexy you can be
When you make up in front of me
Your dazzling face eclipses all
As shining daylight dims the moon.

ANONYMOUS (NEWARI)

She's like a mynah bird
A goddess figurine
Her heels are beautiful
As eggshells freshly peeled
Her calves are beautiful
As cucumbers just picked
Her hips are beautiful
As pillows newly stuffed
Her slit is beautiful
A lamp made from moist clay
Her breasts are beautiful
A fountain's rounded spouts
Her cheeks are beautiful
Two omelettes freshly cooked
Her eyes are beautiful
Two lotus-flowers just plucked
Her face is beautiful
A moon upon the rise.

VARIS SHAH: 'HIR' (PUNJABI)

She walks in beauty

Her lips are scarlet-red as rubies,
her chin a North-grown apple.
Her locks are snakes, which guard a treasure,
her nose a sharp-edge dagger.
Her teeth are jasmine flowers or petals,
or seeds of pomegranate.
She's a picture from Kashmir or China,
a cypress-tree from heaven.
Her neck a crane's, her fingers pods,
on hands as soft as plane-leaves.
Her arms are soft as butter-pats,
her breast is white as marble.
Her bosoms swell like balls of silk,
choice apples form the North.
Her navel is a musk-filled pool,
her lower belly velvet.
Her well-turned buttocks camphor-white,
her thighs fair-fluted pillars.
A sister to the queen of fairies,
she'd stand out in a thousand.
Her lovers swarm like bees around her,
to sacrifice their being.
For love intones from all her features,
its throbbing treble measures.
When once the eyes take up her challenge,
their stake is lost to start with.

WOMEN'S FOLKSONG (RAIASTHANI)

The seven blessings

O my friend, seven blessings have come to our house
To receive them I've spread out the edge of my veil
To the home of my husband great blessings have come.

The first's my garden which waves in the breeze
Where the mangoes are ripe and there's juice in the limes.

The second is in the fair town of my love
Where rich merchants are sitting with lights in their shops.

The next one is outside my dear husband's gate
Where the elephant sways and the horse feeds in peace.

The fourth is within my dear husband's court
Where the groom and the bride will go round the pole.

The fifth is within that kitchen of his
Where the Brahmins are cooking with butter and milk.

The sixth is within that palace of his
Where the windows and balconies sound and smell sweet.

The seventh is found in my dear husband's bed
Where together in love we both laugh as we talk.

KALIDASA: 'RITUSAMHARA' (SANSKRIT)

Hot summer nights

The dark nights broken by the moon
The fountain's cool and dome-shaped spray
The jewels and sweet sandalwood
Are summertime's delights, my dear.

The perfumed palace balconies
The wine-breath from a dear one's lips
The heart-felt songs set to the lute
Give lovers summer nights of joy.

With rounded bottoms clad in silk
With breasts bedecked with sandal paste
With fresh-washed, sweetly fragrant hair
The women soothe their lovers' heat.

Dyed crimson by the *lac*-tree's juice
Their feet are set with ankle-bells
Whose swan-like call at every step
Brings lovers under Cupid's rule.

By draughts from sandal-sprinkled fans
By pearls encircling rounded breasts
By rich sounds form the *veena's* strings
The God of Love is roused from sleep.

All night the moon looks down in lust
Upon the women's faces whom
The palace's cool roof lets sleep
Until abashed by dawn he pales.

FAYADEVA: 'GITAGOVINDA' (SANSKRIT)

Where is he?

He promised but where was he?
My beauty's now quite useless
Oh, who is there to help me?
My friends have all betrayed me.

To meet him in the forest
I went and I was wounded.

To die would be far better
Than suffering these feelings.

This sweet spring night torments me
Another woman's with him.

My jewels and bangles hurt me
I'm set on fire without him.

This garland, even, pains me
Strange symbol of love's arrow.

I wait lost in the jungle
Unthought of and forgotten

In Hari's name I utter
This song to give you comfort.

TWO FOLKSONGS (SANTALI)

Where are their nests?

The birds in the wood are crying, my love
Crying their different songs.

How softly the fish too are crying, my love
Listen, my soul cries for you.

See how at each of the water's four corners
Bright-coloured birds have their nests.

Some fly in the sky and some perch on the branches
Where are their nests, though? Oh, where are their nests?

~ ~

So why did you go to the water, my girl?
So why did you run away from me, my girl?

Dear mother, what can I tell you?
Dear mother, what can I say then?

In Rajaram's garden
The flowers are blooming.

The bushes that bloom there
Have seized me so tightly!

ANONYMOUS (SIRAIKI)

The garden's bare of grass

The garden's bare of grass —
    Where did my lover go?
    I see no track or pass.

With clouds the sky is black —
    Explain to me a plan
    To win my lover back.

The ship sails on the sea —
    Our fates were one till God
    Set you apart form me.

The mangos grow so sweet —
    If he was more aware
    Why should I roam this street?

Three grains of gold will do —
    Who rudely made me wake
    From my sweet dreams of you?

A boat came from the south —
    A sudden special thought
    Left me with open mouth.

The snake writhes in the net —
    Who can be cross with him
    Without whom I'm upset?

ILANKO ATIKAL: 'CILAPPATIKARAM' (TAMIL)

Thinking of her beside the sea

These breaking waves, this beach, these shining sands
These scented flowers, this grove beside the sea
Her fragrant hair, bright face and carp-like eyes
All these have brought distress to me

These conch-shells on the shore, these fragrant groves
These tender petals, these secret haunts of hers
Her fresh young teeth, bright face and youthful breasts
All these have brought distress to me.

How red are the eyes of the girl who is using
Her pestle of coral to pound the white pearls
How red are her eyes, no dark lilies are they
So cruel, so cruel . . .

How red are the eyes of the girl who is swaying
Along like a swan in the grove by the shore
How red are her eyes as she sways like a swan
Like death, like death . . .

How red are the eyes of the girl who is scaring
The birds from the fish with sweet flowers in her hand
How red are her eyes as she scares off the birds
So cruel, so cruel . . .

VEMANA (TELUGU)

Beginnings and endings

When he beholds the beauty of her form
And sees the wavings of her waist-long hair
Who can resist a lovely woman's charms?

Simply to see a lovely woman thrills
Us with a fever which can drive us mad —
Her teeth so flashed in a smile are something else!

Can men who stare at women know them as
They truly are? Desire destroys their sense
Dissolving them like gum that melts in flames.

A man who has feasted and sits at his ease
Has feelings of love at the sight of a woman
For food is the force which inflames his desire.

Both men and women when well-filled with food
Will say that Cupid is tormenting them
But empty stomachs make love powerless.

When love is past, those cherry lips taste like
The nightshade's berry of the poison-nut
Old passion's like the acid mango-leaf.

MIR TAQI MIR: 'MU'AMALAT-E ISHQ' (URDU)

Memories of intimacy

One day my hand was lying on the ground
As we were talking to each other, when
She crushed my finger with her foot and gave
Me pain not empty of delight, and when
I shrieked in agony she massaged it
With long and gentle strokes. (How hard it is
For me now to recall those pleasures past!)
The sight of her would be too much for me
And I would boldly ask: 'Give me this bit!'
She'd smile and say: 'Well, take it, here you are.
I see forbidden fancies fill your brain!'
Without a moment's sadness was I then
Ready to suffer anything from her.
When now I think of her behaviour to me —
What can I say? — I'm overwhelmed by thoughts . . .

One day as she was sitting chewing *paan*
I loved the betel's redness on her lips
And burst out saying: 'If you'd squirt the juice
From your mouth into mine, how glad I'd be!'
'No way!' she said, but I replied: 'How sweet
I'd find the taste of what you've chewed and left!'
She laughed, first put me off, then passed to me
Her lovely leavings. In such gentle ways
As these was she so often kind until
Dark destiny wiped colour from my life.

Irish Love Poems

ANONYMOUS (9TH CENTURY)

He's a Sweetheart

He's a sweetheart
    a nut-filled grove,
Here's a kiss
    to the one I love.

NÍALL MÓR MAC MHUIRICH (1550–1615)

A Long Farewell

A long farewell to last night,
Short-lived night of much pain.
Were I to swing on the gallows tomorrow
I would swallow that draught again.

There are two in this house tonight
And glances speak for the heart,
They may not be lip to lip
But each look pierces like a dart.

There's calumny and slander here,
I'll give them no cause for lies,
But, my dearest darling one,
You may read my eyes.

Keep this night for the two of us,
Let this precious moment stay.
Don't let the morning enter,
Rise, and put out the day!

Oh Virgin Mary, protectress,
Known to be always right,
Come, come and rescue us!
A long farewell to last night.

SEATHRÚN CÉITINN (1570–1650)

Will You Be Sensible, Girl!

Will you be sensible, girl!
And take that hand away;
I'm not the man for the task,
Be love-sick as you may.

Look how my hair is gray,
Bodily I'm unfit,
Even my blood runs slow —
What can you hope from this?

Pray do not think me cruel,
Oh! do not hang your head,
Of course I will always love
You, but not in bed.

Let us break up this kiss,
Tho' it be hard to say,
Let us forbear to touch,
Warmth to desire gives way.

Your curly, clustered poll,
Your eyes more green than dew,
Your fair white rounded breasts,
These are incitements too.

Everything but the one —
Sharing your body's quilt —
I would do for your love,
Everything — short of guilt.

LIAM RUA MAC COITIR (1690–1738)

It's Well For You, Blind Man

It's well for you, blind man,
   women folk you've never seen;
if you had my two eyes
   you'd be as sick as I've been.

God, what a pity I wasn't blind
   before I saw her curling hair
and limber body all of snow —
   oh! my world is bare!

Blind people I used to pity
   before my pain became too much;
pity now has turned to envy
   since being in her clutch.

I pity those who've seen her,
   who don't see her every day;
I pity all ensnared by her
   and those who get away!

Alas for those who go to meet her
   and those she's never known
and those who go to greet her —
   and those she's left alone!

ANONYMOUS (18TH-19TH CENTURIES)

The Coolin

Have you seen the fair-haired lady walking
Along the roads in the bright dew of morning?
Many a blue-eyed youth desires her for his own,
But they will not win her love, for she is mine alone.

And have you seen my dear in the late afternoon
Her arms full of flowers and her hair overflowing?
She is the honeyed promise of summer coming soon,
And every idle fellow dreaming she's his own.

Have you seen her at evening, down beside the shore,
Her gold rings sparkling as she braids her hair?
No wonder Captain Power of the Venus once declared
That he'd give his ship to kiss the lips of one so fair.

The Flowering Sloe

(Abridged)

A pleasant lad gave me a present on market day
And after that a hundred kisses — it's no lie I say;
Woe betide the one who says you're not my love;
And I'd court you in the woods as sure as there's a God above.

A hundred men would have me when they see me drinking ale
But I recall your words and shiver and grow pale;
The mountain side is whitening with the cold blown snow —
And my darling is a fair as the flowering sloe!

Were I a boatman I would hurry across the main
And were I a poet I would write down all my pain:
A pity the dawn won't see us lying down side by side
In some secluded dewy glen — and nothing to hide!

If You Come

If you come at all
Come only at night,
Tread ever so warily
And please don't scare me.
Under the door
You'll find the key
And I'll be alone —
Don't frighten me!

No pot in your way
Not a stool or a can
Or a rope of hay
Not a pin, man!
The dog is so tame
He won't bat an eye —
And where's the shame,
I trained him, didn't I?

Mother's asleep
Dad's hands on her hips,
Kissing her mouth,
Her slow-opening lips.
Ah now, it's fine for her!
But my heart is lead —
Lying on my own
In a feathery bed.

Máirín de Barra

Oh, Máirín de Bara, you have made my mind feeble,
And you've left me sad and lonely, all unknown to my people;
As I lie on my pillow, it's of you I'm always dreaming,
And when I rise in the morning, my heart is still bleeding.

Oh, Máirín, you swept away my sense without warning,
As you knelt in the chapel on Candlemas morning;
Your eyes were far purer than the dewdrops on the barley,
And your voice was far sweeter than the linnet or starling.

I thought I would win you with kisses and coaxing,
I thought you'd be conquered by my promises and boasting;
I was sure that I could charm you as the barley turned golden,
But you left me broken-hearted when the harvest was over.

Oh, happy are the pathways where you stray and you saunter,
And happy are the blackbirds with the melodies you've taught
them;
Oh, happy and thankful are the blankets that warm you,
And how happy for the bridegroom who'll stand beside you at
the altar.

Oh, Máirín, take my warning, don't let any man cheat you,
Stay away from the tailor and beware of his scheming;
As O'Flynn is my name, I swear I'd never ill-treat you,
Oh, clasp me to your heart, love, you'll have your people's
agreement.

Oh, Máirín, if you'd have me, I would walk the world proudly,
I'd take you over the water with no thought of a dowry;
I'd leave my friends and my own people, I'd have no fear of
drowning.
For you'd save me from the grave, love, if you placed your
arms 'round me.

Now I'll drink to your health, love, I'll drink it late and early,
And if we were on the sea, love, I'd drink deep as we were sailing,
If you'd meet me on the quay, love, there's no fear I'd keep you waiting,
And, please God, in a year, love, you could be feeding our baby.

The Red-Haired Man Reproaches His Wife Who Has Left Him

They are saying your little heel fits snugly in the shoe,
They are saying your lips are thin, and saying they kiss well too;
You might have had many's the man, if what they are saying is true.
When you turned your back on your own, but only the tailor would do!

I'd have you know, nine months I was tethered in gaol,
Bolts on my ankles and wrists and a thousand locks on the chain,
And yet, my flight would be swift as the homeward flight of the swan
To spend but a single night with the Wife of the Red-Haired Man!

And I thought, "One home we will share, Beloved, for you and for me,"
And I thought, "'Tis you will sit there and coax my babe on your knee."
Heaven's King's curse be on him who has taken away my good name!
So that lies in the end of it all separate us in shame.

RICHARD BRINSLEY SHERIDAN (1751–1816)

The Geranium

In the close covert of a grove,
By nature formed for scenes of love,
Said Susan, in a lucky hour,
Observe yon sweet geranium flower;
How straight upon its stalk it stands,
And tempts our violating hands:
Whilst the soft bud as yet unspread,
Hangs down its pale declining head:
Yet, soon as it is ripe to blow,
The stems shall rise, the head shall glow.
Nature, said I, my lovely Sue,
To all her followers lends a clue;
Her simple laws themselves explain,
As links of one continued chain;
For her the mysteries of creation,
Are but the works of generation:
Yon blushing, strong, triumphant flower,
Is in the crisis of its power:
But short, alas! its vigourous reign,
He sheds his seed, and drops again;

The bud that hangs in pale decay,
Feels not, as yet, the plastic ray;
To-morrow's sun shall bid him rise,
Then, too, he sheds his seed and dies:
But words, my love, are vain and weak,
For proof, let bright example speak;
Then straight before the wondering maid,
The tree of life I gently laid;
Observe, sweet Sire, his drooping head,
How pale, how languid, and how dead;
Yet, let the sun of thy bright eyes,
Shine but a moment , it shall rise;

Let but the dew of thy soft hand
Refresh the stem, it straight shall stand:
Already, see, it swells, it grows,
Its head is redder than the rose,
Its shrivelled fruit, of dusky hue,
Now glows, a present fit for Sue:
The balm of life each artery fills,
And in o'erflowing drops distills.
Oh me! cried Susan, when is this?
What strange tumultuous throbs of bliss!
Sure, never mortal, till this hour,
Felt such emotion as a flower:
Oh, serpent! cunning to deceive,
Sure, 'tis this tree that tempted Eve;

The crimson apples hand so fair,
Alas! what woman could forbear?
Well, hast thou guessed, my love, I cried,
It is the tree by which she died;
The tree which could content her,
All nature, Susan, seeks the center;
Yet, let us still, poor Eve forgive,
It's the tree by which we live;
For lovely woman still it grows
And in the centre only blows.
But chief for thee, it spreads its charms,
For paradise is in thy arms. —
I ceased, for nature kindly here
Began to whisper in her ear:
And lovely Sue, lay softly panting,
While the geranium tree was planting.
'Till in the heat of amorous strife,
She burst the mellow tree of life.
"Oh Heaven!" cried Susan, with a sigh,
"The hour we taste, — we surely die;
Strange raptures seize my fainting frame,
And all my body glows with flame,
Yet let me snatch one parting kiss
To tell my love I die with bliss:
That pleased, thy Susan yields her breath;
Oh! who would live if this be death!"

THOMAS MOORE (1779–1852)

"At The Mid Hour Of Night . . ."

At the mid hour of night, when stars are weeping, I fly
To the lone vale we loved, when life shone warm in thine eye;
And I think oft, if spirits can steal from the regions of air
To revisit past scenes of delight, thou wilt come to me
there,
And tell me our love is remembered even in the sky.

Then I sing the wild song it once was rapture to hear,
When our voices commingling breathed like one on the ear;
And as Echo for off through the vale my sad orison rolls,
I think, O my love! 'tis thy voice from the Kingdom of
Souls
Faintly answering still the notes that once were so dear.

Did Not

(from *Juvenile Poems, 1801)*

'Twas a new feeling — something more
Than we had dared to own before,
Which then we hid not:
We saw it in each other's eye,
And wished, in every half-breathed sigh,
To speak, but did not.

She felt my lips impassioned touch —
'Twas the first time I dared so much,
And yet she chid not;
But whispered o'er my burning brow,
"Oh, do you doubt I love you now,"
Sweet Soul! I did not.

Warmly I felt her bosom thrill,
I prest it closer, closer still,
Though gently bid not,
Till — oh! the world hath seldom heart
Of lovers, who so nearly erred,
And yet, who did not.

SAMUEL LOVER (1797–1868)

Rory O'More;

(Or, All For Good Luck)

Young Rory O'More courted Kathleen bawn —
He was bold as a hawk, she as soft as the dawn;
He wished in his heart pretty Kathleen to please,
And he thought the best way to do that was to tease.
"Now Rory, be aisy!" sweet Kathleen would cry,
Reproof on her lips, but a smile in her eye —
"With your tricks, I don't know, in troth, what I'm about;
Faith! you've tazed me till I've put on my cloak inside out."
"Och! jewel," says Rory, "That same is the way
Ye've thrated my heart for this many a day;
And 'tis plazed that I am, and why not, to be sure?
For 'tis all for good luck," says bold Rory O'More.

"Indeed, then," says Kathleen, "don't think of the like,
For I half gave a promise to soothering Mike:
The ground that I walk on he loves, I'll be bound — "
"Faith," says Rory, "I'd rather love you than the ground."
"Now, Rory, I'll cry if you don't let me go;
Sure I dream every night that I'm hating you so!"
"Och," says Rory, that same I'm delighted to hear,
For dhrames always go by conthraries, my dear.
So, jewel, keep dhraming that same till ye die,
And bright morning will give dirty night the black lie!
And 'tis plazed that I am, and why not, to be sure!
Since 'tis all for good luck," says bold Rory O'More.

"Arrah, Kathleen, my darlint, you've tazed me enough;
Sure I've thrashed, for your sake, Dinny Grimes and Jim Duff;
And I've made myself, drinking your health, quite a baste —
So I think, after that, I may talk to the praste."
Then Rory, the rogue, stole his arm round her neck,
So soft and so white, without freckle or speck;
And he looked in her eyes, that were beaming with light,
And he kissed her sweet lips — don't you think he was right?
"Now, Rory, leave off, sir — you'll hug me no more —
That's eight times to day that you've kissed me before."
"Then here goes another," says he, "to make sure!
For there's luck in odd numbers," says Rory O'More.

HELEN LADY SELINA DUFFERIN (1807–1867)

Katey's Letter

Och, girls dear, did you ever hear I wrote my love a letter?
And although he cannot read, sure, I thought 'twas all
the better
For why should he be puzzled with hard spelling in
the manner,
When the meaning was so plain that I loved him faithfully?
I love him faithfully —
And he knows it, oh, he knows it, without one word from me.

I wrote it, and I folded it and put a seal upon it;
'Twas a seal almost as big as the crown of my best bonnet —
For I would not have the postmaster make his remarks upon it,
As I said inside the letter that I loved him faithfully,
I love him faithfully —
And he knows it, oh, he know it without one word from me.

My heart was full, but when I wrote I dare not put the half in;
The neighbors know I love him, and they're mighty fond
of chaffing,
So I dared not write his name outside for fear they would
be laughing,
So I wrote "From little Kate to one whom she loves faithfully."
I love him faithfully —
And he knows it, oh, he knows it, without one word from me.

Now, girls, would you believe it, that postman's so consated,
No answer will he bring so long as I have waited —
But maybe there may not be one for the reason that I stated,
That my love can neither read no write, but he loves me
faithfully,
He loves me faithfully —
And I know where'er my love is that he is true to me.

CHARLES DAWSON SHANLEY

Kitty Of Coleraine

As beautiful Kitty one morning was tripping
  With a pitcher of milk, from the fair of Coleraine,
When she saw me she stumbled, the pitcher it tumbled,
  And all the sweet buttermillk watered the plain.
"O, what shall I do now? — 't was looking at you now!
  Sure, sure such a pitcher I'll ne'er meet again!
'T was the pride of my dairy: O Barney M'Cleary!
  You're sent as a plague to the girls of Coleraine."

I sat down beside her, and gently did chide her,
  That such a misfortune should give her such pain.
A kiss then I gave her; and ere did I leave her,
  She vowed for such pleasure she'd break it again.

  'T was hay-making season — I can't tell the reason —
Misfortunes will never come single, 't is plain;
  For very soon after poor Kitty's disaster
The devil a pitcher was whole in Coleraine.

JOHN BOYLE O'REILLY (1844–1890)

A White Rose

The red rose whispers of passion,
  And the white rose breathes of love;
O, the red rose is falcon,
  And the white rose is a dove.

But I send you a cream-white rosebud
  With a flush upon its petal tips;
For the love that is purest and sweetest
  Has a kiss of desire on the lips.

GEORGE MOORE (1852–1933)

Rondo

(from Flowers of Passion, 1878)

Did I love thee? I only did desire
To hold thy body unto mine,
And smite it with strange fire
Of kisses burning as a wine,
And catch thy odorous hair, and twine
It thro' my fingers amorously.
        Did I love thee?

Did I love thee? I only did desire
To watch thine eyelids lilywise
Closed down, and thy warm breath respire
As it came through the thickening sighs;
And seek my love in such fair guise
Of passions' sobbing agony.
        Did I love thee?

Did I love thee? I only did desire
To drink the perfume of thy blood
In vision, and thy senses tire
Seeing them shift from ebb to flood
In consonant sweet interlude,
And if love such a thing not be,
        I loved not thee.

WILLIAM COX BENNETT

The Worn Wedding-Ring

Your wedding-ring wears thin, dear wife; ah, summers not
a few,
Since I put it on your finger first, have passed o'er me
and you;
And, love, what changes we have seen, — what cares and
pleasures, too, —
Since you became my own dear wife, when this old ring
was new!

O, blessings on that happy day, the happiest of my life,
When, thanks to God, your low, sweet "Yes" made you my
loving wife!
Your heart will say the same, I know; that day's as dear to
you, —
That day that made me yours, dear wife, when this old ring
was new.

How well do I remember now your young sweet face that day!
How fair you were, how dear you were, my tongue could
hardly say;
Nor how I doted on you; O, how proud I was of you!
But did I love you more than now, when this old ring
was new?

No — no! no fairer were you then that at this hour to me;
And, dear as life to me this day, how could you dearer be?
As sweet your face might be that day as now it is, 'tis true;
But did I know your heart as well when this old ring was new?

O partner of my gladness, wife, what care, what grief is there
For me you would not bravely face, with me you would
not share?
O, what a weary want had every day, if wanting you,
Wanting the love that God made mine when this old ring
was new!

Years bring fresh links to bind us, wife, — young voices that
are here;
Young faces round our fire that make our mother's yet
more dear;
Young loving hearts your care each day makes yet more like
to you,
More like the loving heart made mine when this old ring
was new.

And blessed be God! all he has given are with us yet; around
Our table every precious life lent to us still is found.
Though cares we've known, with hopeful hearts the worst
we've struggled through;
Blessed be his name for all his love since this old ring
was new!

The past is dear, its sweetness still our memories treasure yet;
The griefs we've borne, together borne, we would not
now forget.
Whatever, wife, the future brings, heart unto heart still true,
We'll share as we have shared all else since this old ring
was new.

And if God spare us 'mongst our sons and daughters to
grow old,
We know his goodness will not let your heart or mine
grow cold.
Your agéd eyes will see in mine all they've still shown to you,
And mine in yours all they have seen since this old ring
was new.

And O, when death shall come at last to bid me to my rest,
May I die looking in those eyes, and resting on that breast;
O, may my parting gaze be blessed with the dear sight of you,
Of those fond eyes, — fond as they were with this old ring
was new!

KATHERINE TYNAN (1861–1931)

The Return

I rested in your easy chair,
 Slept in your late-abandoned bed
And felt your pleasure everywhere,
 A benediction on my head,
Through sleep and waking: all the while
I was quite sure I felt your smile.

I knelt and laid my cheek upon
 The cushions that you lately pressed;
All your familiar things forgone
 Took to my own use and behest,
Quite sure your spirit leant to bless
Your daughter in that loneliness.

I sat beside your fire aglow,
 In the dim hours 'twixt night and day,
And knew you would be glad to know,
 You who gave everything away —
I had your old room, sweet and warm,
Safe from the winter night and storm.

I slept, I rose, I rested there;
 My thoughts, my dreams were still and glad.
The dear room kept its happy air
 As in the golden years we had;
And sleeping, waking, all the while
I was quite sure I felt your smile.

WILLIAM BUTLER YEATS (1865–1939)

The Lover Mourns For The Loss Of Love

Pale brows, still hands and dim hair,
I had a beautiful friend
And dreamed that the old despair
Would end in love in the end:
She looked in my heart one day
And saw your image was there;
She has gone weeping away.

O Do Not Love Too Long

Sweetheart, do not love too long:
I loved long and long,
And grew to be out of fashion
Like an old song.

All through the years of our youth
Neither could have known
Their own thought from the other's
We were so much at one.

But O, in a minute she changed —
O do not love too long,
Or it will grow out of fashion
Like and old song.

When You Are Old

When you are old and gray and full of sleep,
And nodding by the fire, take down this book,
And slowly read, and dream of the soft look
Your eyes had once, and of their shadows deep;

How many loved your moments of glad grace,
And loved your beauty with love false or true;
But one man loved the pilgrim soul in you
And loved the sorrows of your changing face.

And bending down beside the glowing bars
Murmurs, a little sadly, how love fled
And paced upon the mountains overhead
And hid his face amid a crowd of stars.

For Anne Gregory

'Never shall a young man,
Thrown into despair
By those great honey-colored
Ramparts at your ear,
Love you for yourself alone
And not for your yellow hair.'

'But I can get a hair-dye
And set such color there,
Brown, or black, or carrot,
That young men in despair
May love me for myself alone
And not for my yellow hair.'

'I heard an old religious man
But yesternight declare
That he had found a text to prove
That only God, my dear,
Could love you for yourself alone
And not for your yellow hair.'

PÁDRAIG PEARSE (1880–1916)

Ideal

Naked I saw thee,
O beauty of beauty!
And I blinded my eyes
For fear I should flinch.

I heard thy music,
O sweetness of sweetness!
And I shut my ears
For fear I should fail.

I kissed thy lips
O sweetness of sweetness!
And I hardened my heart
For fear of my ruin.

I blinded my eyes
And my ears I shut,
I hardened my heart
And my love I quenched.

I turned my back
On the dream I had shaped,
And to this road before me
My face I turned.

I set my face
To the road here before me,
To the work that I see,
To the death that I shall meet.

JAMES JOYCE (1882–1941)

She Weeps Over Rahoon

Rain on Rahoon falls softly, softly falling,
Where my dark lover lies.
Sad is his voice that calls me, sadly calling,
At grey moonrise.

Love, hear thou
How soft, how sad his voice is ever calling,
Ever unanswered and the dark rain falling,
Then as now.

Dark too our hearts, O love, shall lie and cold
As his sad heart has lain
Under the moongrey nettles, the black mould
And muttering rain.

VALENTIN IREMONGER (b. 1918)

Hector

Talking to her, he knew it was the end,
The last time he'd speed her to sleep with kisses:
Achilles had it in for him and was fighting mad.
The roads of his longing she again wandered,
A girl desirable as midsummer's day.

He was a marked man and he knew it,
Being no match for Achilles whom the Gods were backing.
Sadly he spoke to her for hours, his heart
Snapping like sticks, she on his shoulder crying.
Yet, sorry only that the meaning eluded him.

He slept well at night, having caressed
Andromache like a flower, though in a dream he saw
A body lying on the sands, huddled and bleeding,
Near the feet a sword in bits and by the head
An upturned, dented helmet.

CHRISTY BROWN (1932–1981)

What Her Absence Means

It means
   no madcap delight will intrude
into the calm flow of my working hours
   no ecstatic errors perplex
my literary pretensions.

It means
   there will be time enough for thought
undistracted by brown peril of eye
   and measured litany of routine deeds
undone by the ghost of a scent.

It means
   my neglect of the Sonnets will cease
and Homer come into battle once more.
   I might even find turgid old Tennyson
less of a dead loss now.

It means
   there will be whole days to spare
for things important to a man —
   like learning to live without a woman
without altogether losing one's mind.

It means
   there is no one now to read my latest poem
with veiled unhurried eyes
   putting my nerves on the feline rack
in silence sheer she-devil hell for me.

It means
  there is no silly woman to tell me
"Take it easy — life's long anyway —
don't drink too much — get plenty of sleep — "
  and other tremendous clichés.

It means
  I am less interrupted now with love.

Italian Love Poems

ANONYMOUS (c. 1200)

Sicilian Love Songs

Send no messages, for they are lies;
Send no messages, for they are sin;
No message save the uplifting of the eyes;
No message save your glance that comes to win
The knowledge of my lips how red they be.
Ah, men are bats, fair hues no husbands see!

More than honey the words you speak are sweet,
Honest and wise, nobly and wittily said,
Yours are the beauties of Camiola complete,
Of Iseult the blonde and Morgana the fairy maid.
If Blanchefleur should be added to the group,
Your loveliness would tower above each head.
Beneath your brows five beautiful things repose:
Love and a fire and flame, the lily, the rose.

PIER DELLA VIGNA (c. 1200–1249)

Love

Love, in whom I wish and hope, has
given me, my beauty, the reward of you.
I save myself, waiting for good weather
and season, until my hope becomes real:
as a man who is on the sea waits for
good weather to continue his voyage
and spreads his sails at the right time,
and that hope never deceives him; I do
the same, my Lady, to come to you.

If I could come to you now, my love,
like a thief at night and never be seen!
It would be such joyous luck for me,
if love were to do me so great a favor.
I would be so eloquent, love, and tell you
that I have loved you for so long, more
sweetly than Pyramus love Thisbe,
and I will love you as long as I live.

My love of you makes me desire,
and gives me hope and great joy,
for I do not care if I suffer or have
sorrow if I can think of the moment
when I shall come to you; if I delay
too long, my fragrant love, it seems
I would die and that you will lose me.
So my beauty, if you love me, watch
over me lest I die hoping for you.

I live hoping for you, my lady, and
now I ask my heart back from you,
and it seems late for love to bring me
to your heart; and I watch for the time
that you will favor my hope, when I may
spread my sails towards you, my rose,
and rest my heart in your secure harbor.

GUIDO CAVALCANTI (1240–1300)

Sonnet 1

You, who do breach mine eyes and touch the heart,
 And start the mind from her brief reveries,
 Might pluck my life and agony apart,
 Saw you how love assaileth her with sighs,
And lays about him with so brute a might
 That all my wounded senses turn to flight.
 There's a new face upon the seigniory,
 And new is the voice that maketh loud my grief.
Love, who hath drawn me down through devious ways,
 Hath from you noble eyes so swiftly come!
 'Tis he who hath hurled the dart, wherefrom my pain,
First shot's resultant! and in flanked amaze
 See how my affrighted soul recoileth from
 That sinister side wherin the heart lies slain.

DANTE ALIGHIERI (1265–1321)

The New Life: Canzone 1 (1-14)

Ladies that have an intelligence in love,
Of mine own lady I would speak with you;
Not that I hope to count her praises through,
But telling what I may, to ease my mind.
And I declare that when I speak thereof
Love sheds such perfect sweetness over me
That if courage failed not, certainly
To him my listeners must all be resigned.
Wherefore I will not speak in such large kind
That mine own speech should foil me, which were base;
But only will discourse of her high grace
In these poor words, the best that I can find,
With you alone, dear dames and damsels;
'Twere ill to speak thereof with any else.

The Divine Comedy: Canto 5

When I replied, my words began: "Alas,
how many gentle thoughts, how deep a longing,
had led them to this agonizing pass!"
Then I addressed my speech again to them,
and I began: "Francesca, your affliction
moves me to tears of sorrow and of pity.
But tell me, in the time of gentle sighs,
with what and in what way did Love allow you
to recognize your still uncertain longings?"
And she to me: "There is no greater sorrow
than thinking back upon a happy time
in misery, and this your teacher knows.
Yet if you long so much to understand
the first root of our love, then I shall tell
my tale to you as one who weeps and speaks.

One day, to pass the time away, we read
of Lancelot, how love had overcome him.
We were alone, and we suspected nothing.
And time and time again that reading led
our eyes to meet, and made our faces pale,
and yet one point alone defeated us.
When we had read how the desired smile
was kissed by one who was so true a lover,
this one, who never shall be parted from me,
While all his body trembled, kissed my mouth.
A Gallehault indeed, that book and he
who wrote it, too; that day we read no more."
And while one spirit said these words of pity to me,
the other wept, so that, because of pity,
I fainted, as if I had met my death.
And then I fell as a dead body falls.

FRANCESCO PETRARCA (1304–1374)

The Wind and Earth and Heavens Rest

Now while the wind and earth and heavens rest,
  While sleep holds beast and feathered bird in fee
  And high above a calm and aweless sea
  The silent stars obey the night's behest,
Lie awake and yearning, sore distressed
  And racked by thoughts of my sweet enemy,
  Yet though her face recalled brings death to me
  'Tis only with such dreams I soothe my breast.
So from one living fountain, gushing clear,
  Pour forth alike the bitter and the sweet,
  And one same hand can deal me good or ill.
Whence every day I die anew of fear
  And live again to find that hope's a cheat,
  And peace of heart and mind escapes me still.

GIOVANNI BOCCACCIO (1313–1375)

The Decameron, Day 2

Love, if I can get free from your claws, I can
hardly imagine any other hook will ever take me.

I entered into your war when I was young, thinking
it would be the sweetest and highest peace, laying
my arms on the ground, as confidently as
one who trusts; vicious, deceitful, dishonorable
tyrant, you who seized me immediately
with your arms and cruel claws.

Then, tangled in your chains you held me captive,
full of tears and grief, to him who was born for my
death, and he has me in his thrall, and he is such
a cruel master and he has never been moved,
not even once, by my sighing and weeping.

The wind hears all my prayers to him; he will
no listen to me or consider my pleas; thus my
anguish increases each day, so that living is
tedious, but yet I cannot die; O grieve master,
for my sake, bring about what I cannot do;
deliver him to me in your bonds.

If you will not do this, at least release me
from the ties bound by hope, I beg you,
master, please; because if you do, I feel
sure I shall become beautiful again, as I
used to be, and when sorrow has been
lifted from me I shall dress myself with
white and crimson flowers.

LORENZO DE' MEDICI (1449–1492)

I Saw My Lady by a Cool, Fresh Stream

I saw my lady by a cool, fresh stream
  Among green branches and gay ladies stand;
  Since the first hour when I felt love's hot brand
  I never saw her face more lovely gleam.
This sight fulfilled in part my fondest dream
  And over my soul put reason in command;
  But when I left, my heart stayed at her hand,
  My fears and grief the greater came to seem.
When now the sun bent downwards to the west,
  And left the earth in shadow and in night,
  Then my own sun was hidden from its ray.
The setting sun more sadness brought at best.
  How all too little lasts this world's best light!
  But memory does not soon fade away.

ANGELO POLIZIANO (1454–1494)

I Thank You, Love

I thank you, Love,
for every pain and torment,
and I am happy now for every sorrow.

I am happy for what I have suffered,
Master, in your marvelous kingdom; since
in your kindness, so undeserving, you have
given me such a promise, since you have
made me worthy of such a blessed smile
that has carried my heart to paradise.
I thank you, Love.

Those lovely eyes have carried my heart
to paradise, where I saw you, Love, hidden
in your growing flames. O shining eyes
that have taken my heart, where do
you obtain such sweet power?
I thank you, Love.

I doubted for my life; but my lady
dressed in white saved me with a loving
smile, happy, beautiful and modest. Her
hair was decked with roses and violets,
her eyes surpassed the sun in brightness.
I thank you, Love.

LUDOVICO ARIOSTO (1474–1533)

Orlando Furioso, Chapter 8

O night, more clear and shining, sweeter,
happier and more fortunate than day, so
much dearer that I hardly expected you.
Stars that attempt to hide love's thefts
that have dimmed your lights, not by you
were the friendly shadows broken.

Timely sleep, that leaving two lovers
alone, had overcome everyone else,
that I was almost invisible.
Kind door, that was opened with
a muffled sound so soft that he who
was close by hardly heard a sound.

O mind, uncertain if it dreamed or not,
when I saw myself held by my goddess
and my mouth was enclosed in hers.
O blessed hand, that leads me next,
O quiet steps that go before me.
O room that locked me in secure.

O repeated embraces, that bind hips,
breast, neck with so many twines that
the ivy or acanthus have no more.
Mouth, from which I sup ambrosia,
not ever satiated, O soft tongue, O dew,
in which I bathe and soften my burnt heart.

Breath, which inhales far more pleasant
fragrances than the phoenix on his pyre
on which he flames and dies.
O bed, witness to my pleasures;
bed, cause of my tasting a sweetness
that I do not envy the gods their nectar.
All of you, one by one, shall I keep in my
everlasting eternal memory as ministers of
pleasure and I praise you with all my power.

TORQUATO TASSO (1544–1595)

I Love You Because

I love you simply because you are fair,
and my stars desire it
not that I hope for anything from you,
my sweet life, except misery.

And if you decide to show pity
sometimes for my eyes,
I do not hope for anything but
weeping for so much sadness.

Nor, because you hear my burning sighs,
that for you I allow the winds to hear,
does this heart of mine hope for
anything from you but sorrow.

Let me still love you and look on you
and sigh for you, since
sadness, weeping and sorrow are
the only rewards I have for my love.

UGO FOSCOLO (1778–1827)

On Himself

So that the rattling of the chain may be silent,
I live on tears, on hope, on love and silence;
for tenderness restrains me, if I speak with her,
or think or write of her. You alone listen to
me, oh lonely stream, where every night Love
leads me in his company, here I confide my
tears and pour out my sufferings, and here
confide in you the fullness of my sorrow.

And tell how those laughing eyes burnt my
heart with an immortal ray, how her mouth,
so like a rose, and the shimmering fragrant
locks of her hair, and the whiteness of her arms,
and her sweet voice taught me to weep for love.

GIACOMO LEOPARDI (1798–1837)

First Love (1-30)

I remember the first day when
I fought the battle of love, I said:
Alas, if this is love, I grieve!
My eyes downcast, staring,
I wondered how my innocent heart
ventured into this new realm.

Ah, how wrongly you ruled me, Love!
Why should sweet emotion
lead to such longing and such pain.
Torn apart, thwarted, and never calm,
filled with sorrows and despair,
still my heart drowned in delight.

Tell me of your anguish, loving heart,
your horror at such a thought
each happiness turns to weary anxiety.
All day long, that thought remained,
and at night, driven by desire,
when the world around seemed quiet

You were restless, happy and miserable.
I tossed and turned, fatigued on my bed,
and never stopped trembling.
Sad and afraid and exhausted,
I closed my eyes:
feverish dreams kept me from sleep.

How clearly out of the dark
her tender image appeared; my eyes
sealed I saw her on my closed eyelids.
How subtle were these confused emotions
that wandered through my consciousness.

VINCENZO CARDARELLI (1887–1960)

The Adolescent (1-31)

Upon you, adolescent virgin,
a sacred shadow seems to rest.
Nothing is more mysterious
and adorable and unique
than your flesh disrobed.
But you seclude yourself in careful dress,
and with your gracefulness
live in some distant land,
unaware of who will reach you there.
Surely not I. If I behold you walking by,
at such a queenly distance,
with your locks unbound
and your body straight,
vertigo sweeps me away.
You are the impenetrably smooth creature
in whose breathing stirs
the dark bliss of flesh that scarcely
can withstand its plenitude.

If the blood which fans out wide
in flames upon your face,
the cosmos has its laughter
as in the black eye of a swallow.
Your pupil is seared
by the sun within it.
Your mouth is locked tight.
Those white hands of yours do not know
the shameful sweat of handled flesh.
And I think of how your body,
tortuous and eager,
causes love to despair
in the heart of man!

CAMILLO SBARBARO (1888–1967)

Now That You Have Come

Now that you have come,
dancing into
my life
a guest in a closed room —
to welcome you, love longed for so long,
I lack the words, the voice,
and I am happy just in silence by your side.

The chirping that deafens the woods
at dawn, stills
when the sun leaps to the horizon.

But my unrest sought you,
when, as a boy,
on summer nights I came
stifled to the window:
for I didn't know, and it worried my heart.
And yours are all the words
that came, like water brimming over,
unbidden to my lips,
the desert hours, when childishly
my adult lips rose
alone, longing for a kiss . . .

ALBINO PIERRO (b. 1916)

I Love You

"My love for you is as big as the world,"
you tell me happily, and I believe you;
and I watch you in the air, a rosy
feather on the brazier's breath.

Do you notice, love, that I'm not crying
in your arms but shouting for gladness?
I bless the day that I was born,
that has drowned me now in so much beauty.

I enter into your eyes, like sunlight
in the leaves when it is day.
and there I find not one remaining cross
and even the night is always noon.

Then, hand in hand, together we enter,
who knows just where or how, into heaven;
we see the blazing of a fire, and we can hear
the candle dying in the flame.

The dark has been too deep, too many the thorns
that pierced us through; now the air
will be forever radiant, and in our hearts
we'll hear only one single voice.

"Love" is what that voice will say;
the world has become so beautiful,
no one is unhappy anymore,
and the stars are no longer cold in the sky.

Japanese Love Poems

ANONYMOUS FRONTIER GUARD (8TH CENTURY)

While the leaves of the bamboo rustle
On a cold and frosty night,
The seven layers of clobber I wear
Are not so warm, not so warm
As the body of my wife.

Lady Heguri

A thousand years, you said,
as our hearts melted.
I look at the hand you held,
and the ache is hard to bear.

BASHO (1644–1694)

Finis

Having sucked deep
In a sweet peony,
A bee creeps
Out of its hairy recesses.

Jewish Love Poems

Love Poems from Hebrew Sources

UNKNOWN MEDIEVAL POET

Ode to a Bridegroom

Rejoice, O bridegroom, in the wife of thy youth, thy comrade!
Let thy heart be merry now, and when thou shalt grow old
Sons to thy sons shalt thou see, thine old age's crown;
Sons who shall prosper and work in place of their pious sires.
Thy days in good shall be spent, thy years in pleasantness.
Floweth thy peace as a stream, riseth thy worth as its waves,
For peace shall be found in thy home, rest shall abide in thy
dwelling.
Blessed be each day's work, blessed be thine all,
And thy bliss this assembly shall share, happy in thee.
By grace of us all ascend, thou and thy goodly company;
Rise we, too, to our feet, lovingly to greet thee;
One hope is now in all hearts, one prayer we utter,
Blessed be thy coming in, blessed be thy going forth.

RACHEL

His Wife

She turns and calls him by name,
And her voice is as always;
While I in my voice am unsure,
It might give me away.

She passes by in the street,
Alongside him; In front of him,
Out front. While I, in the
Darkness of evening, hide.

She has a ring of gold —
It sparkles, and is peaceful.
While my chains of iron
Hold me ever fast.

PROVERBS 31:10-31

A Woman of Valour

A woman of valour who can find?
For her price is far above rubies.
The heart of her husband doth safely trust in her,
And he hath no lack of gain.
She doeth him good and not evil

All the days of her life.
She seeketh wool and flax,
And worketh willingly with her hands.
She is like the merchant ships;
She bringeth her food from afar.
She riseth also while it is yet night,
And giveth food to her household,
And a portion to her maidens.
She considereth a field, and buyeth it;
With the fruit of her hands she planteth a vineyard.
She girdeth her loins with strength,
And maketh strong her arms.
She perceiveth that her merchandise is good;
Her lamp goeth not out by night.
She layeth her hands to the distaff,
And her hands hold the spindle.
She stretcheth out her hand to the poor;
Yea, she reacheth forth her hands to the needy.
She is not afraid of the snow for her household;
For all her household are clothed with scarlet.
She maketh for herself coverlets;
Her clothing is fine linen and purple.
He husband is known in the gates,
When he sitteth among the elders of the land.
She maketh linen garments and selleth them;
And delivereth girdles unto the merchant.
Strength and dignity are her clothing;
And she laugheth at the time to come.
She openeth her mouth with wisdom;
And the law of kindness is on her tongue.
She looketh well to the ways of her household,
And eateth not the bread of idleness.
Her children rise up, and call her blessed;
Her husband also, and he praiseth her:
'Many daughters have done valiantly,
But thou excellest them all.'
Grace is deceitful, and beauty is vain;
But a woman that feareth the Lord, she shall be praised.
Give her the fruit of her hands;
And let her works praise her in the gates.

SONG OF SONGS II: 4-5

Banquet Room

He brought me to the banquet room
and his banner of love was over me.
Sustain me with raisin cakes,
Refresh me with apples
For I am faint with love.

Behold, Thou Art Fair

Behold, thou art fair, my love; behold, thou art fair;
Thine eyes are as doves behind thy veil;
Thy hair is as a flock of goats,
That trail down from mount Gilead.
They teeth are like a flock of ewes all shaped alike,
Which are come up from the washing;
Whereof all are paired,
And none faileth among them.
Thy lips are like a thread of scarlet,
And thy mouth is comely;
Thy temples are like a pomegranate split open
Behind thy veil.
Thy neck is like the tower of David
Builded with turrets,
Whereon there hang a thousand shields,
All the armour of the mighty men.
Thy two breasts are like two fawns
That are twins of a gazelle,
Which feed among the lilies.
Until the day break,
And the shadows flee away,
I will get me to the mountain of myrrh,
And to the hill of frankincense.
Thou art all fair, my love;
And there is no spot in thee.

SONG OF SONGS VII: 11–14

I Am My Beloved's

I am my beloved's,
And his desire is toward me.
Come, my beloved, let us go forth into the field;
Let us lodge in the villages.
Let us see whether the vine hath budded,
Whether the vine-blossom be opened,
And the pomegranates be in flower;
There will I give thee my love.
The mandrakes give forth fragrance,
And at our doors are all manner of precious fruits,
New and old,
Which I have laid up for thee, O my beloved.

SONG OF SONGS VIII: 6-7

Set Me as a Seal Upon Thy Heart

Set me as a seal upon thy heart,
As a seal upon thine arm;
For love is strong as death,
Jealousy is as cruel as the grave;
The flashes thereof are flashes of fire,
A very flame of the Lord.
Many waters cannot quench love,
Neither can the floods drown it;
If a man would give all the substance of his house for love,
He would utterly be contemned.

CHAIM NACHMAN BIALIK

Famished Eyes

These eyes are famished and they plead so long,
These lips are thirsty, clamorous to kiss,
These beauties of desire for dalliance,
These hidden love delights like the Abyss
Know not when sated.

And with carnality, riot of joy,
And with flesh sensual, voluptuous,
From pleasure mountains blessed I am cloyed;
Ah! beauty, could you know the languorous soul you
have wearied.

No storm has swept my passions, I was clean,
Till beauty breathed her spirit and defiled
A simple lad, brought pitiless to your feet —
A perfect heart, a crystal mind, a child empty of blossom.

Small moment's boundless happiness was mine,
I blessed the hand that hurt, of sad bliss made,
In that small moment's happy, happy joy
A full world crashed about me — great wealth paid for
all your flesh!

The Golden Peacock

The golden peacock flies away,
Where are you flying, pretty bird?
I fly across the sea.
Please ask my love to write a word,
To write a word to me!
I know your love, and I shall bring
A letter back, to say,
With a thousand kisses, that for spring
He plans the wedding day.

One Two Three

One two three four five six seven eight
    Marry your girl before it's too late.
Do not reflect, do not delay,
    Or someone else will snatch her away.
Once I had honey, and did not eat,
    And another came and found it sweet.
There were two sisters — one was fair,
    The second was dark, and dark her hair.
They were both lovely and good to see,
    And I love them both equally.
I pondered and pondered with aching head.
    I couldn't decide which to wed.
Months passed and still I could not see
    Which I should ask my wife to be.
Till alas two devils came one day,
    And carried both of them away.
Now I am old and sick and worn,
    Broken-hearted and forlorn.
And I say to all who will listen to me,
    Don't let your lives like my life be.
One two three four five six seven eight
    Marry your girl before it's too late.
Do not reflect, do not delay,
    Don't let another snatch her away.

SAUL TCHERNICHOVSKY

With This Ring . . .

With this ring I thee charm in the rite
Of the butterfly born to its world,
To its life of one day, the bridal night
Of one hour amid colored wings.
With this ring I thee charm in the plight
Of choirs of mosquitoes that dance
In the forest clearing, in the light
Of their mute song of noon's fiery romance.

With this ring I thee charm in the rite
Of the rustling tree and the plants
Fluttering in the breeze, that recite
In the tongue of aromas and speak only scents.
With this ring I thee charm in the ways
Of that great yearning that sings,
The great yearning so silent always,
That blossoms again every year, every spring.

With this ring I thee charm in the rite
Of the bellowing deer that broods,
In longing for a mate, at twilight,
With glowing horns at the edge of the woods.
With this ring I thee charm with the power
Of all the might in animal essence,
Of worlds once destroyed and reborn in the roar
Of all the thousands of tribes of existence.

With this ring I thee charm, in the deep
Secret of all the poems of man and his song.
Of his magician's words, of the glories that sleep
In the mysteries of his faith, hidden so long
In the guess and the stress of each human heart,
In the source of his dance and the base of his art.
Bewitched, now be still — and never depart —
I thee charm thee forever . . . till death us do part.

MOSES IBN EZRA (1055–1138)

Your Rightful Portion

Caress the breasts of the lovely girl at night,
And kiss the lips of the beautiful girl all day long.
Spurn those who chide you for loving,
Who counsel you to their own advantage.
Heed my words of truth: There is no life
But in the company of beauty's daughters,
Who stole out of Eden to torture the living,
And there is no man living who is not full of desire.
Plunge your heart into pleasures;
Make merry, drink out of wine-skins by the
Riverside to the sound of lyres, doves and swifts.
Dance and rejoice, clap your hands, get drunk,
And knock on the door of the lovely girl!
These are the delights of the world,
Take your part (as did the priests) from
The ram of installation. Always allot yourself
The very portion that was your leaders' due;
Do not stop sipping the moist lips until you hold
Your rightful portion — the breast and the thigh!

JUDAH HALEVI (c. 1085–1140)

A Slave to Love

By the life of our troth, my love,
By your life and the life
Of Love which has shot an arrow at me,
Truly I have become a slave to Love,
That has pierced my ear,
That has cut my heart in two.

Awake, My Fair

(To her sleeping love)

Awake, my fair, my love, awake,
That I may gaze on thee!
And if one fain to kiss thy lips
Thou in thy dreams dost see,
Lo, I myself then of my dream
The interpreter will be.

The Fair Maiden

The night when the fair maiden revealed the likeness of her
form to me,
The warmth of her cheeks, the veil of her hair,
Golden like a topaz, covering
A brow of smoothest crystal —
She was like the sun making red in her rising
The clouds of dawn with the flame of her light.

Ophra

Ophra washes her clothes in the waters
Of my tears; And spreads them out in the sunshine of
her radiance.
She requires no water from the fountains — she has my
two eyes
And no need for sunshine but her own beauty.

Parting

If parting be decreed for the two of us,
Stand yet a moment while I gaze upon thy face . . .
By the life of love, remember the days of thy longing,
As I remember the nights of thy delight.
As thine image passeth into my dreams,
So let me pass, I entreat thee, into thy dreams,
Between me and thee roar the waves of a sea of tears
And I cannot pass over unto thee.
But O, if thy steps should draw nigh to cross —
Then would its waters be divided at the touch of thy foot,
Would that after my death unto mine ears should come
The sound of the golden bells upon thy skirts!
Or shouldst thou be asking how farest thy beloved, I from the
depths of the tomb
Would ask of thy love and thy welfare
Verily, to the shedding of mine heart's blood
There be witnesses, thy cheeks and thy lips.
How sayeth thou it is not true, since these be my witnesses
For my blood, and that shine hands have shed it?
Why desirest thou my death, whilst I but desire
To add years unto the years of thy life?
Thou, thou dost rob my slumber in the night of my longing,
Would I not give the sleep of mine eyes unto thy eyelids? . . .
Yea, between the bitter and the sweet standeth my heart —
The gall of parting, and the honey of thy kisses.

After thy words have pounded my heart into thin plates,
Thine hands have cut it into shreds.
It is the likeness of rubies over pearls
What time I behold thy lips over thy teeth.
The sun is on thy face and thou spreadest out the night
Over his radiance with the clouds of thy locks.
Fine silk and broidered work are the covering of thy body,
But grace and beauty are the covering of shine eyes.
The adornment of maidens is the work of human hands,
But thou — majesty and sweetness are thine adornment . . .
In the field of the daughters of delight, the sheaves of love
Make obeisance unto thy sheaf . . .
I cannot hear thy voice, but I hear
Upon the secret places of my heart, the sound of thy steps
On the day when thou wilt revive
The victims whom love for thee hath slain — on the day when
  thy dead shall live anew,
Then turn again to my soul to restore it to my body;
  for on the day
Of thy departure, when thou wentest forth, it went out
  after thee.

Love Poems from Yiddish Sources

SONG OF SONGS I:2–17

Let Him Kiss Me

Let him kiss me with the kisses of his mouth
For thy love is better than wine.
Thine ointments have a goodly fragrance;
Thy name is an ointment poured forth;
Therefore do the maidens love thee.
The king has brought me into his chambers,
We will be glad and rejoice in thee.
We will find thy love more fragrant than wine.
Sincerely do they love thee.
Draw me, we will run after thee.
I am black, but comely,
O ye daughters of Jerusalem,
As the tents of Kedar,
As the curtains of Solomon.
Look not upon me that I am swarthy,
That the sun has tanned me;
My mother's sons were incensed against me,
They made me keeper of the vineyards, but my own
  vineyard have I not kept.
O tell me, thou whom my soul loveth,
Where thou feedest, where thou makest thy flock to
  rest at noon,
For why should I be as one that veileth herself
Beside the flocks of thy companions?
If thou know not, O thou fairest among women,
Go thy way forth by the footsteps of the flock
And feed thy kids, beside the shepherds' tents.

I have compared thee, O my love,
To a steed in Pharaoh's chariots.
Thy cheeks are comely with circlets, thy neck with
  beads.
We will make thee circlets of gold
With studs of silver.
While the king sat at his table
My spikenard sent forth its fragrance.
My beloved is unto me as a bag of myrrh,
That lies between my breasts.
My beloved is unto be as a cluster of henna
In the vineyards of Ein Gedi.
Behold, thou art fair, my love, behold, thou art fair.
Thine eys are as doves.
Behold, thou art fair, my beloved, yea pleasant.
Also, our couch is cushioned.
The beams of our house are cedars,
And our panels are cypresses.

A. ALMI

To the Little Girl

I write these words to the little girl in the little post office:
When you took the letter from me and stamped it, and I in haste
quickly murmured "Thank you" — you surely did not know that you
had stamped the mark of that little station on my heart.
And surely you did not know that in the moment when your finger
touched my hand when you took the letter, everything in that letter
became a lie — for in that moment all the bitterness I had breathed
into the words of the letter fell from my heart, and turned into a
wonderfully pleasing feeling.
And surely you did not know that I who — I thought — had long been
free of boyish sentiment, in that mysterious moment became a boy
in love again, who dreams, awake, of a girl's eyes, fingers, hair.
And now when I am far from you, the center of the whole world — no,
of the whole universe! — has become a small station somewhere in
Canada, where a small post office stands, in which a
little girl sits, who takes letters from hurrying passengers stopping
awhile at the station, and disappearing soon behind a cloud of smoke.

MORRIS ROSENFELD

Too Late

I would have loved you,
But I cannot.
I would have loved you,
But I do not burn.
My fire, it has cooled off,
Beloved; I am played out.

It was too late when you became good
I have already lost my desire.
Now you cry:
"I love you so!"
It's too late, my child
Too late, my gold.

Why were you silent before?
When I sought to have you.
The wind carried my plea.
Too late, my child
It's just too late!

When I begged you with tears,
You did not want to hear.
Now you cry your eyes blind.
To late, my child
Too late for me!

We love only when we can,
The fire cannot burn forever,
It goes out quickly.
It's your payment:
Too late, my child,
Too late, my gold.

ABRAHAM SUTZKEVER

Here I Am

Here I am, now fully grown
Stung with song by a raging bee
I heard your call to me in the dawn's light
And through night and dawn and sweat I came.
Towns and villages broke away from me,
A flash of lightning shone on my old gray home,
Rain washed away the red trail,
And I stood still at the sound of your name,
As before, the blue mirror of conscience,
My hands, like branches stripped bare
Bang swiftly at you shiny door,
My eyes stare with wonder and
Are drawn to you like a sail,
But suddenly the open door
And you are not here,
Everything has flown away,
You are not here.
A song remains,
A silly cry,
A not knowing why.

J. L. TELLER

Desire

Irritated, pillows torture
A girl's raw nipples.
Her mouth is hard as stone
Yet moist with early fog.
Her head pounds tom-toms,
Burning and dull.
Her hands, like nettles,
Scorch the naked body.

Love Poems from Ladino Sources

LADINO LOVE SONG

Loving You

Loving you is like rising to the clouds
In worlds reached only by imagination.
Loving you is like flying in the sky
In the radiant light of a dawning day.
Loving you is really living.

Un Tarde De Verano

One afternoon in summer
I passed through the Moorish quarter
And saw a Moorish maiden washing
At the foot of a cold fountain.
I said to her: Lovely Moor,
I said to her: Beautiful Moor
Give water to my horse
From these crystaline waters.
I am not a Moor, Knight
I was born in France.
I was captured by the Moors
On Easter Sunday.
Do you wish me to take you to France?
With my horse I would do so.
And the clothes, Knight
Where would I leave them?
Those of silk and wool
Take with you.
Those which are useless
Throw in the river.
And my honor, Knight
With whom would I leave that?
I swear not to touch it
Until you are mine.
Upon arriving at the mountains
The lovely young woman sighed and cried.
Why do you cry, lovely young woman
Why do you cry, beautiful one?

Mexican Love Poems

OCTAVIO PAZ (b. 1914)

Counterparts

In my body you search the mountain
for the sun buried in its forest.
In your body I search for the boat
adrift in the middle of the night.

Last Dawn

Your hair lost in the forest,
your feet touching mine.
Asleep you are bigger than the night,
but your dream fits within this room.
How much we are who are so little!
Outside a taxi passes
with its load of ghosts.
The river that runs by
                    is always
running back.

Will tomorrow be another day?

Touch

My hands
Open the curtains of your being
Clothe you in a further nudity
Uncover the bodies of your body
My hands
Invent another body for your body.

Persian Love Poems

HĀFIZ (c. 1300–1388)

The lips of the one I love are my perpetual pleasure:
The Lord be praised, for my heart's desire is attained.

O Fate, cherish my darling close to your breast:
Present now the golden wine-cup, now the rubies of those lips.

They talk scandal about us, and say we are drunks —
The silly old men, the elders lost in their error.

But we have done penance on the pious man's behalf,
And ask God's pardon for what the religious do.

O my dear, how can I speak of being apart form you?
The eyes know a hundred tears, and the soul has a
hundred sighs.

I'd not have even an infidel suffer the torment your beauty
has caused
To the cypress which envies your body, and the moon that's
outshone by your face.

Desire for your lips has stolen from Hāfiz' thought
His evening lectionary, and reciting the Book at dawn.

Rudaki

Came to me —
        Who?
She.
        When?
In the dawn, afraid.

        What of?
Anger.
        Whose?
Her father's.
        Confide!

I kissed her twice.
        Where?
On her moist mouth.
        Mouth?
No.
        What, then?
Cornelian.
        How was it?
Sweet.

Polish Love Poems

ANONYMOUS

A Wife

So much did I love my wife before we tied the knot
That I could have eaten her up right on the spot;
Now when the days go by without even a kiss,
I regret most sincerely that I had not done this.

MALCHER PUDLOWSKI (b. 1588?)

To My Eyes

Naughty eyes, why do you look there
    Where danger and harm both say beware?
She chained mey up most maliciously
    Taking my priceless freedom away from me.
She took my heart, which one can't deny,
    And who loses his heart, truly does die.
So don't look in her direction anymore
    If true love's union cannot be, or
Make her give her heart to replace mine;
    Else let her return the heart she did confine.
For it's completely useless and quite shoddy
    To have my heart without my body.

JAN ANDRZEJ MORSZTYN (1621–1693)

To His Mistress

Your sweet eyes are not eyes, but radiance of the sun
  Before whose dazzling light all reason is undone;
Your sweet lips are not lips, but coral, soft and red,
  That binds our every sense with bonds of crimson thread.
Your breasts are not breasts, but shapes divinely bright
  That capture our warm will in fetters of delight.
Thus reason, sense and will are slaves to the behests
  Of light and hue and form in eyes and lips and breasts.

To a Butterfly

Beware, butterfly! There is danger in fire!
  Watch out for the candle and that bright face,
  In which death glows in ornamental grace,
  And your torments do not so readily acquire.

You hurry to your own death, one most treacherous,
  You make your own end, as your dreams are filled
  Of securing salvation by what will have you killed.
  — Ah, poor suitor, you've already perished thus!

But in this you achieved your pleasure's end
  And are happy and suffer no remiss —
  For you parted company with your loved light.

Oh! If I could also similarly for her extend,
  She who burns my heart, dazzles my sight,
  And die after giving her a first and final kiss!

A Smart Maid

"When is the best time to be courted," a girl asked a doctor,
"in the morn or the evening?"
And the doctor answered: "It will make the evening sweeter,
but in the morning it's not bad for the health."
"I will do as you say," she replied; "in the evening
for taste, in the morning for health."

To Walek

You have your clothes to yourself, your estates too,
And your profits and bags full of money are all
meant for you;
You have ponds, herds, gardens and groves to admire as
your own,
And exceptional manners and high morals are
solely yours to be sown;
You alone possess great knowledge hidden from public view,
Only your wife has been shared with at least a
dozen or two.

IGNACY KRASICKI (1735–1801)

A Perfect Marriage

Thank God! I saw a marriage old-fashioned and rare,
A couple very happy, full of kindness and of care.
A gentle love it was, the wonder of many already a 'beding;
Too bad that the husband died a week after the wedding!

ADAM MICKIEWICZ (1798–1855)

Good Morning

Good morning! I dare not wake her, lovely sight!
Her spirit has in part flown to paradise,
In part stayed here, her divine face revives,
As the sun part in sky, part in cloud that's white.

Good morning! Now she sighs, her eyes shine with light,
Good morning! Now the sun offends her eyes,
Her lips are annoyed by the frolicsome flies,
Good morn! Sun at the window, I by your side.

I brought sweeter good morn, but your sleepy charms near,
Have disarmed my boldness; let me first learn:
Do you rise with kind heart? Are you of good cheer?

Good morning! You won't let me kiss your hand then?
You tell me to go, I go, your clothes are here,
Dress and come out soon — I'll say good morning again.

I Speak to Myself

I speak to myself, with others I falter,
My heart beats fiercely, I become breathless,
I feel sparks in my eyes, my face is bloodless,
Strangers ask loudly if my health's in order

Or something about my mind they whisper.
When I fall on my bed after day's distress,
Hoping that in sleep my suffering I'll suppress,
My heart kindles in my mind fiery specters.

I start, I run, I put the words together,
With which I want to curse your ruthlessness,
That formed a million times, I fail to remember.

But when I see you, I cannot express
Why I'm calm again, cool as flint my manner,
Just to burn anew — as of old be speechless.

Uncertainty

While I don't see you, I don't shed a tear;
I never lose my senses when you're near;
But, with our meetings few and far between
There's something missing, waiting to be seen.
Is there a name for what I'm thinking of?
Are we just friends? Or should I call this love?

As soon as we have said our last good-byes,
Your image never floats before my eyes;
But more than once, when you have been long gone,
I seemed to feel your presence linger on.
I wonder than what I've been thinking of:
Are we just friends? Or should I call this love?

When I'm downcast, I never seek relief
By pouring out my heart in tales of grief;
Yet, as I wander aimlessly, once more
I somehow end up knocking at your door;
What brought me here? What am I thinking of?
Are we just friends? Or should I call this love?

I'd give my life to keep you sound and well,
To make you smile, I would descend to hell;
But though I'd climb the mountains, swim the seas
I do not look to be your health and peace:
Again I ask, what am I thinking of?
Are we just friends? or should I call this love?

And when you place your hand upon my palm,
I am enveloped in a blissful calm,
Prefiguring some final, gentle rest;
Be still my heart beats loudly in my breast
As if to ask: what are you thinking of?
Are you two friends? or will you call this love?

Not bardic spirit seized my mortal tongue
When I thought of you and composed this song;
But still, I can't help wondering sometimes:
Where did these notions come from, and these rhymes?
In heaven's name, what I was dreaming of?
And what had inspired me? Friendship or love?

Conversation

My love! what need we have of talk?
Why when I want my feelings to share,
I can't just let my soul to yours declare!
Why must it be crumbled to words
Which before they reach your ears and your heart
Will wither on my lips, and in the air fall apart?

I love you — a hundred times I keep on saying,
But you grieve and start to sting,
Complaining that my love I'm not able
To completely say, state, sing;
And in this weary state I have no doubt
I can't give a sign of life before I give out.

I've tired my lips with such vain misuse;
Now I want to join them to yours in amour's abysses,
And our talk to be only with beating hearts —
And passioned sighs and kisses.
And for hours, days, years thus converse
To the end of this world, and the universe.

IN THE ALPS AT SPLÜGEN, 1829

To***

No, never, you will never let me be!
You follow me on land, across the sea,
I watch your footsteps sparkle and then fade
On frozen Alpine lakes; in the cascade
I hear your voice or else I sense you near,
And look behind with longing and with fear.

Ungrateful! In these peaks, so stern and proud,
Which from their depths rise up to pierce a cloud,
I tire of eternal ice and snow,
And pause as my own tears begin to flow;
I seek the Northern Star in misty blue
And Lithuania, your small house, and you.
Ungrateful! Perhaps now, queen of the ball,
You hold your merry, laughing guests in thrall
By telling tales of our long-past romance;
Or do you conquer new hearts as you dance?
Are you content now that you are adored
By your meek subjects, by that servile horde?
That pleasure wakes you, that you're lulled by bliss?
Is there, then, nothing from the past you miss?
And wouldn't you be far happier, my dear,
Sharing your outcast's wanderings, being here?
I'd lead you by the hand amid these crests,
And with my songs I'd ease your weariness.
I'd plunge first into every stream we meet
To gather stones so that your dainty feet
Could cross the streams and never touch the foam.
I'd warm your hands with kisses; we'd call home
Some rustic shepherd's hut along the way,
Where we'd rest from the hardships of the day.
Wrapped in my cloak beside the fireplace
You'd fall asleep and wake in my embrace.

Spin Love

from *The Lausanne Lyrics*

Spin love just as a worm spins silk thread from inside,
And pour it from your heart as springs from bedrocks flow,
And spread it, frail as sheets of gold, hammered out wide
From glittering seeds; and let it stream below and ride
With rivers underground, and blow high as winds blow;
And scatter it like grains , which take deep root and grow;
Nurse it for mankind as a mother does her child!

And herewith grows your might — at first, like that of nature,
Then might exceeding all the elements; then vast
As power born of ceaseless generation;
Then might of humankind; of angels; and, at last,
Might rivaling the Lord of All Creation.

GABRYELLA (1819–1876)

Fancy Flights

He. I'll take a candle, lantern and a burning brand,
To search if there's an honest girl in the land.

She. I'll take the moon, the stars — I'll take the bright sun,
To find a man with loving heart — perhaps there's one.

He. I have looked, I have searched, till convinced in the matter,
To find a good girl man must shake his gold at her.

She. I've looked with persistence, and it's plain to be seen
That men can love deeply — love themselves, I mean.

He. I have found one very honest — one I could adore;
Quiet and pretty — a painted doll in a store.

She. After much painstaking I've found the one I thought,
A handsome, merry warrior, but on a canvas wrought.

He. Just let the painted doll show feeling in her eyes,
The warrior might to horseback from canvas arise.

She. If the young warrior on the horseback sat
He might find the painted doll's heart went pit-a-pat.

KAZIMIERZ PRZERWA-TETMAJER (1865–1940)

[I Look for You . . .]

I look for you — and when I see you
I pretend that I don't see you.

I love you — and when I meet you
I pretend that I don't love you.

I will die because of you — and before I die
I will cry out that I'm dying just by chance . . .

BOLESLAW LESMIAN (1878–1937)

In the Darkness

Bodies know in whom they reside
When in darkness they lie side by side.
Lips and hands most intimate —
Night passes over them with regret.
The world stays, but in such hesitancy;
The trees rustle, but beyond their density.
And over the forest in a farther place
God moves both wind and space.
And the wind says, as the guest:
"I won't return tonight to this forest!" —
The forest darkens, while the stars beatify,
While over the sea, white gulls fly.
One says: "I saw the writing on the star!"
And the other: "I saw the heavens way afar!" —
But the third one is silent, for it saw
Two bodies in the darkness glowing in amorous awe.
The darkness, which touched the closeness there,
Found nothing but caresses sweet and bare!

MARIA MORSTIN-GORSKA (1893–1972)

Coming Home

I am coming home in the evening
among tenements positioned at odd angles —
shadows of bare trees tremble
on a cold, heartless pavement.

I walk and walk — I am not thinking of you;
to constantly think of you is not possible —
there are so many other things in the world
so many other things, so many other people . . .

I look up and see the moon journeying
across a clear, peaceful sky —
but my shadow is moving ahead of me,
as it hurries, hurries — to you.

KONSTANTY ILDEFONS GALCZYNSKI (1905–1953)

A Lyrical Conversation

"Tell me, how do you love me?"
"Very well."
"Go on."
"I love you in the sun. And by candlelight.
I love you in a hat and in a beret.
In a strong wind on the highway, and at a musical play.
Amongst the lilacs and birch trees, and raspberries and
maple trees
And when you sleep. And when you work hard.
And when you beat an egg with impressive command —
even when the spoon falls from your hand.
In a taxi. In a car. Without exception.
At the end of a street. At its intersection.
And when you part your hair with a comb.
In danger. And on a merry-go-round.
At sea. In the mountains. In galoshes. In bare feet.
Today. Yesterday. And tomorrow. Day and night.
And in the spring, when the sky is full of swallows' flight."
"And how do you love me in the summer?"
"Like the essence of summer."
"And when there are clouds and changeable moods in the fall?
"Even when you lose your parasol."
"And when the winter silvers the window-frames?"
"I love you in the winter like a joyful flame.
Near your heart. Right by its side.
With snow outside the window. And crows on the snow."

Portuguese Love Poem

LUIS DE CAMOËNS

Dear gentle soul, who went so soon away
Departing from this life in discontent,
Repose in that far sky to which you went
While on this earth I linger in dismay.
In the ethereal seat where you must be,
If you consent to memories of our sphere,
Recall the love which, burning pure and clear,
So often in my eyes you used to see!

If then, in the incurable, long anguish
Of having lost you, as I pine and languish,
You see some merit — do this favour for me:
And to the God who cut your life short, pray
That he as early to your sight restore me
As from my own he swept you far away.

Roman Love Poems

Korean Love Tales

CATULLUS (84–54 B.C.)

Poem 5

My Lesbia, let us live and love
And care not the least for old men
Who sermonize and disapprove.
Suns when they sink can rise again,
But we, when our brief light has shone,
Must sleep through the long night.
Kiss me a thousand kisses, then
A hundred more, then a second
Thousand and hundred, and now
Thousands and hundreds more
And we lose count of how many
And nobody can do evil to us
By keeping count of our kisses.

HORACE (65–8 B.C.)

Book 1, Ode 5

What slender youth, covered with perfumes
Embraces you among the myriad roses
In the pleasant grotto, O Pyrrha?
For who do you tie up your hair

With such simple elegance? How often
Shall he lament the fickle faith and gods,
And wonder at rough waters in a stormy gale,
He who now embraces you,

As he fondly sees you in a golden aura,
Who hopes that you will be free of passion
For another, and always beautiful, ignorant
He who knows not the treacherous breeze.

Wretched ones to whom you, untried, now
Appear so dazzling. As for me, the temple
With its votive tablet shows I have hung up
My garments to the god, master of the sea.

Book 1, Ode 13

When you, O Lydia, praise
the rosy neck of Telephus,
or his waxen arms, my heart
swells with an angry passion.

My senses take leave of reason
and my complexion pales, while
a moist tear glides down my cheek
proving the lingering fires of my love.

I burn to think how, mad with wine,
that boy has harmed your gleaming
shoulders, or in a state of frenzy he
left his teeth marks on your lips.

If you had heeded me, you would not
hoped for constancy from that one
who savagely profanes the sweet lips
that Venus has imbued with nectar.

Three times blessed and more are they
who are united with an unbroken bond;
no wretched quarrels shall ever separate
our love before the final days of life.

PROPERTIUS (50–16 B.C.)

Book 2, Poem 15 (1-16)

O happy me! O night has shone for me! And O you
my darling bed made blessed by my delight.
What happy words we shared beside the lamp
And how happily we struggled when the light was out!

For now she wrestled me with her bare breasts
And closed her tunic and teased me with delay.
With a kiss she opened my eyes, heavy with sleep,
And whispered, "How can you sleep, lazybones!"

How often our arms slipped into new embraces.
How long my kisses lingered on her sweet lips.
Venus is spoiled by serving her in darkness,
Surely you know that sight is the path of love.

PETRONIUS (c. A.D. 5–65)

That Long Night

That long night will be dear to us, Nealce,
when you first laid your head on my breast:
The bed, and the couch, and the silent lamp
that saw you come softly to do your pleasure
are all so dear. Come then, let us endure even
though we have grown older and enjoy these
years which will soon pass. It is quite proper
to prolong our love as we grow old. Grant that
what we began in such haste, not end in haste.

At Rest in Bed

I had just gone to bed and begun to enjoy the silence
of the night and sleep was slowly overcoming my eyes.
When savage Love jerked me up by the hair and threw
me about and commanded me to stay up all night.
He said, "You are my slave, the lover of a thousand
girls, have you become so tough that you can lie
here all alone?" I jumped up in my barefeet and got
half dressed and ran off in all directions, and went
nowhere by any of them. First I ran, then I lingered
and I am now ashamed to be wandering the streets.
The voice of men, the roar of carts, the songs of birds,
even the barking of the dogs, everything was still, and
me alone, afraid of my bed and sleep, ruled by lust.

CARMINA BURANA (c. 1150 A.D.)

Juliana by the Greenwood Tree

One sweet spring Juliana
stood under the greenwood tree
in the company of the sister
        Sweet love!

Who could pass you by at such a time!

The trees blossom now
and the birds lasciviously sing,
virgins' pure thoughts take flight.
        Sweet love!

The lilacs bloom again
and the maidens in the vale
sing of the high god's power.
        Sweet love!

Could I embrace the one I love,
and underneath the forest's leaves
I would kiss her with such pleasure.
        Sweet love!

Blossoming Flowers

Flowers blossom to their peak
and bedeck the world with colors,
and the grass becomes green again.

May young men, about to love,
hold in reverence and respect
the avowals they pursue.

Grant that Venus may hear
those who call upon her and
send Cupid to be present.

May she allow the young men
who are earnest in their quest
to succeed in finding their love.

Venus, even through old, but
always young, sets her shafts
to flights of love in young girls.

She arms all lovers for contest
but never hinders the boys nor
allows the girls to be harmed.

JOANNES SECUNDUS (1512–1536)

The Thirteenth Kiss

Faint from our sweet encounter, love, I lay
panting; my languid fingers play on your neck.
The passion was all consuming, my lips were dry,
I could hardly breathe, I saw death before me.
I saw the waves of Styx roll before my eyes,
I saw old Charon waiting on the far shore,
I was trembling in the bottom of my heart
Until your kisses brought me back to life,
And bid the ferryman to wait no longer
But sail back to the shore without me.

I was wrong, I do not mean without me,
I am but a shade in the land of the living.
The feeble soul that dwells within my body
Is a part of you and will forever strive to
Break away from its fragile abode and flee
To its own place in the company of death.
And were it not for your love, my darling
I would leave limbs to the care of darkness.
Come, let your lips join my lips and let
Us bring our souls together in one breath,
Until, as the passion ebbs and begins to flow
As a single stream of life from two bodies.

The Seventeenth Kiss

As the red rosebud unfolds its dewy petals
When night begins to fade into rosy morning,
So do the lips of my lady welcome the day
Bedewed by me with kisses though the night.
As the cherry tree blossoms in white and red
After spring has gone but before summer appears
So do her cheeks appear as the new blossoms
Of snow-white violets held in a virgin's hand.
O miserable me! Your kisses burn my heart,
Why must I be forced to leave your side?
Let those lips remain like roses all day long
When evening brings you to my bed again.
But if another lover should seek your lips,
May your lips grow paler than my cheek.

The Prelude

Let others sing of the cruelties of war,
all of the carnage and dying heroes,
who shed their blood twice for fame.
I want only one death. I would rather
write verses telling how Cupid draws
his arrows on me to prove is power.

Even as I spoke, the boy drew near,
with bow and arrows and his torch,
his wings were quivering bright in the sky.
I trembled and grew pale with frights,
for I thought I saw him sharpening
his arrows on a whetstone for me.

Fire and Ice

Lydia hit my heart with a ball of snow
and soon ignited a fire within my soul.
This was a most strange manner to
start a flame with this frozen water.
But so it was. How can I live at ease,
when I am trapped by such perils?
There is no cold to quench such a fire;
must be vanquished with another flame.
A mutual warmth is my only salvation;
Come now Lydia and burn with me.

Russian Love Poems

VASILY ZHUKOVSKY (1783–1859)

You were before me,
Standing in silence;
Your face was downcast
And deep in thought.
It made me think of
The past we loved so.
That was the last time
It saw this world here.
Away you vanished,
A silent angel.
Today your grave is
Quiet as heaven.
There all things earthly
Are thoughts of heaven.
Stars of the sky,
Silence of night!

ALEXANDER PUSHKIN (1799–1837)

When I embrace
your slender forms
And tender words
Of love and praises
Pour out to you
In exultation,
In silence from my tight embrace
You free yourself
And answer
With a mistrustful smile;
Your memory has promptly stored
Of all the stories of treacheries,
And you are sad and wearied
with all the words of promises and rapture . . .
I denounce all the cunning tricks
Of my wicked youth,
And expectations of the meetings
In silence of the nightly gardens,
Sweet talking in the silent darkness.
I denounce the seductive passion of my verses,
And fond caresses of frivolous girls,
Their tears and moaning
That always came too late.

A Burnt Letter

Farewell, letter of love! Farewell: she has bade.
I lingered for a long time! For long I hesitated
To burn in fire all my joy.
But now it is time. Burn, the letter, burn.
I am ready; my soul is numb.
Your leaves are licked by the greedy flame . . .
A moment! They are ablaze! Aflame! And then
Thin coils of smoke drift up,
interweave with my prayers
And vanish. The melted wax seethes and looses
The last traces of my seal-ring. O Providence!
All gone! The darkened sheets curl up;
Upon the heap of ashes the cherished outlines
Show white . . . My Chest feels tight. O precious ashes,
The poor comfort of my crestfallen fate,
Stay always near my heart . . .

YEVGENY BARATYNSKY (1800–1844)

The Kiss

That kiss you gave me, soft and light,
Pursues me in my fancy still.
Through noisy day, through quiet night
I feel your touch, I feel its thrill!

I fall asleep, my eyes I close
And dream of you, and dream of bliss.
Deceptive joy! — the sweet dream goes,
To leave but love and weariness.

MIKHAIL LERMONTOV (1814–1841)

When absent, I have much to say,
But crave your voice alone; when near:
So stern your eyes, I turn away,
Confused, in silence and in fear.
I do not hear to reach your mind,
Or touch with artless words your heart.
It seems amusing, but I find
defeat and grief my fated part.

Gratitude

I am grateful to you for everything,
For passions' long torments,
For bitterness of tears and poison of kiss,
For vengeance of enemies and slander of friends;
For the passion of my heart, wasted in the desert,
For all with which I have been deceived.
Grant only one wish, that from now on
I will not be grateful to you much longer.

INNOKENTY ANNENSKY (1856–1909)

Two Loves

There is a love like smoke: if cramped,
It stupefies; give it freedom and, and
It will be gone . . . To be like
Smoke, but eternally youthful . . .

There is a love like a shadow: by day
It lies at your feet, it heeds you:
At night it embraces you soundlessly . . .
To be as a shadow, together night and day.

ALEXANDER BLOK (1880–1921)

What long-forgotten gleam is this?
An instant, through the violining
I catch a different strain beginning!
That low, deep voice of her it is.

Of her, my friend of old, replying
To my first love; and I recall
It always on the days when fall
The snowstorms, blusterously flying;

When traceless melts the past, and when
'Tis only alien passions tell me,
Tell me a little, now and then,
Of happiness that once befell me.

SERGEI GORODETSKY (1884–1957)

The Birch Tree

I fell in love with you one yellow-amber day,
When born by every graceful branch
A delightful languor
Trickles slowly along the bright azure sky.

Your body was as white as foam
Of choppy waves of a lake
When the wind the lake caresses.
While a happily laughing Lel* pulls out
The rays of your long black tresses.

The Sun, Yarila** placed his bright crown
Over the top of your verdant hair,
And twined and interwove with all the blue
That green in radiant azure.

* *Lei — a shepherd (also the old Pagan Slavic spirit of love)*
** *Yarila — the Slavic pagan Sun God*

ANNA AKHMATOVA (1889–1966)

The little cloud was up in the sky
Like a spread out fleece of a grey squirrel.
He said: "I am not sorry that your body,
Will melt in March, my fragile Snow Maiden."

My hands turned cold inside a fluffy muff.
Fear and confusion came to the heart.
O how can I retrieve those fleeting weeks
Of his love, so short and so capricious.

I want no bitter feeling, nor revenge,
May I decease with the last white snow.
I asked the cards about him on the Twelfth-Night Eve
I was already his friend in January.

He loved three things alone:
White peacocks, evensong,
Old maps of America.
He hated children crying,
And raspberry jam with his tea,
And womanish hysteria.
. . . And he had married me.

MARINA TSVETAYEVA (1892–1941)

This tenderness — how to explain it?
I've touched other locks and many,
I've touched other locks, and darker,
More burning lips known than yours.

The stars rose and sank above me.
(This tenderness — how to explain it?)
The stars rose and sank. Above me
Pressed close to the singer's breast.

This tenderness — how to escape it?
How flee from it, sly young hopeful,
You singer with silky lashes
Who happened to pass this way?

KONSTANTIN SIMONOV (1915–1979)

Wait for me and I'll come back,
Wait and I'll be back.
Wait through tedium yellow rains.
Wait through snow haze.
Wait through unbearable summer gaze,
Wait when the others wait not,
Wait when no letters you'll get,
Wait when there will be no hope
Wait when all others will give up.

Wait for me and I'll come back . . .

Scottish Love Poems

ANONYMOUS

Kiss'd Yestreen

Kiss'd yestreen, and kiss'd yestreen,
Up the Gallowagate, down the Green:
I've woo'd wi' lords, and woo'd wi' lairds
I've mool'd wi' carles and mell'd wi' cairds,
I've kiss'd wi' priests — 'twas done i' the dark,
Twice in my gown and thrice in my sark;
But priest, nor lord, nor loon can gie
Sic kingly kisses as he gae me.

mool'd = played
mell'd= meddled
sark=shirt

Lord Randal

'O where hae ye been, Lord Randal, my son?
O where hae ye been, my handsome young man?'
'I hae been to the wild wood; mother, make my bed soon,
For I'm weary wi' hunting, and fain wald lie down.'

'Where gat ye your dinner, Lord Randal, my son?
Where gat ye your dinner, my handsome young man?'
'I din'd wi' my true-love; mother, make my bed soon,
For I'm weary wi' hunting, and fain wald lie down.'

'What gat ye to your dinner, Lord Randal, my son?
What gat ye to your dinner, my handsome young man?'
'I gat eels boil'd in broo; mother, make my bed soon,
For I'm weary wi' hunting, and fain wald lie down.'

'What became of your bloodhounds, Lord Randal, my son?
What became of your bloodhounds, my handsome young man?'
'O they swell'd and they died; mother, make my bed soon,
For I'm weary wi' hunting, and fain wald lie down.'

'O I fear ye are poison'd, Lord Randal, my son!
O I fear ye are poison'd, my handsome young man!'
'O yes! I am poison'd; mother, make my bed soon,
For I'm sick at the heart, and I fain wald lie down.'

O Gin My Love Were Yon Red Rose

O gin my love were yon red rose,
That grows upon the castle wall,
And I myself a drap of dew
Into her bonny breast to fall;
O then, beyond expression blest,
I'd feast on beauty all the night,
Seal'd on her silk-saft falds to rest,
Till fley'd away by Phoebus' light!

fley'd=frightened

ANONYMOUS, TRANSLATED FROM GAELIC

The Dart of Love

The dart of love as piercing flies
As the seven-grooved spear to fling;
Brown maiden of the liquid eyes,
Warm as my plaid the love I bring.

The damsel there who sang to sweet,
She in a chair of gold demure,
A silken carpet 'neath her feet,
Myself I blessed her face so pure.

Sweet are the birds beside the sea,
Sweet are the swans upon the mere,
Sweeter my lover's voice to me
When a song she pours in mine ear.

O'er the meadows on a calm day
Sweeter than mavis unto me
My lover's voice, a ho, a hey,
Beautiful maid my love is she.

Sweeter to me her kissing lip
Than the honey and the spruce-tree beer,
Though we twain the mead were to sip
From two glasses together here.

ROBERT BURNS (1759–1796)

Ae Fond Kiss

Ae fond kiss, and when we sever, —
Ae fareweel, and then — for ever!
Deep in heart-wrung tears I'll pledge thee!
Warring sighs and groans I'll wage thee!

Who shall say that fortune grieves him,
While the star of hope she leaves him?
Me, nae cheerfu' twinkle lights me, —
Dark despair around benights me.

I'll ne'er blame my partial fancy,
Naething could resist my Nancy;
But to see her was to love her —
Love but her, and love for ever.

Had we never lov'd sae kindly —
Had we never lov'd sae blindly —
Never met — or never parted,
We had ne'er been broken-hearted!

Fare-thee-weel, thou first and fairest!
Fare-thee-weel, thou best and dearest!
Thine be ilka joy and treasure,
Peace, Enjoyment, Love, and Pleasure!

Ae fond kiss, and then we sever!
Ae fareweel, alas! for ever!
Deep in heart-wrung tears I'll pledge thee!
Warring sighs and groans I'll wage thee!

A Red, Red Rose

O my luve is like a red, red rose
  That's newly sprung in June.
O, my luve is like the melodie,
  That's sweetly play'd in tune.

As fair art thou, my bonnie lass,
  So deep in luve am I,
And I will luve thee still, my dear,
  Till a' the seas gang dry.

Till a' the seas gang dry, my dear
  And the rocks melt wi' the sun!
And I will love thee still, my dear,
  While the sands o' life shall run.

And fare thee weel, my only luve,
  And fare thee weel a while!
And I will come again, my luve,
  Tho it were ten thousand mile!

It is Na, Jean, thy Bonie Face

It is na, Jean, thy bonie face
   Nor shape that I admire;
Altho' thy beauty and thy grace,
   Might weel awauk desire:
Something, in ilka part o' thee,
   To praise, to love, I find;
But dear as is thy form to me,
   Still dearer is thy mind.

Nae mair ungen'rous wish I hae,
   Nor stronger in my breast,
Than, if I canna mak thee sae,
   At least to see thee blest.
Content am I, if Heaven shall give
   But happiness to thee:
And as wi' thee I'd wish to live,
   For thee I'd bear to die.

Ye Banks and Braes

Ye banks and braes o' bonie Doon,
How can ye bloom sae fresh and fair!
How can ye chant, ye little birds,
And I sae weary fu' o' care!
Thou'll break my heart, thou warbling bird,
That wantons thro' the flow'ring thorn,
Thou minds me o' departed joys,
Departed, never to return.

Oft hae I rov'd by bonie Doon,
To see the rose and woodbine twine;
And ilka bird sang o' its Luve
And fondly sae did I o' mine;
Wi' lightsome heart I pu'd a rose,
Fu' sweet upon its thorny tree;
And my fause Luver staw my rose,
But, ah! he left the thorn wi' me.

JAMES HOGG (1770–1835)

Love is Like a Dizziness

Chorus

O, Love, love, love!
Love is like a dizziness;
It winna let a poor body
Gang about his biziness!

The Moon Was A-waning

The moon was a-waning,
  The tempest was over;
Fair was the maiden,
  And fond was the lover;
But the snow was so deep,
  That his heart it grew weary,
And he sunk down to sleep,
  In the moorland so dreary.

Soft was the bed
  She had made for her lover,
White were the sheets
  And embroider'd the cover;
But his sheets are more white,
  And his canopy grander,
And sounder he sleeps
  Where the hill foxes wander.

Alas, pretty maiden,
  What sorrows attend you!
I see you sit shivering,
  With lights at your window;
But long may you wait
  Ere your arms shall enclose him,
For still, still he lies,
  With a wreath on his bosom!

How painful the task
  The sad tidings to tell you! —
An orphan you were
  Ere this misery befell you;
And far in yon wild,
  Where the dead-tapers hover,
So cold, cold and wan
  Lies the corpse of your lover!

SIR WALTER SCOTT (1771–1832)

Woman's Faith

Woman's faith, and woman's trust —
Write the characters in dust;
Stamp them on the running stream,
Print them on the moon's pale beam,
And each evanescent letter
Shall be clearer, firmer, better,
And more permanent, I ween,
Than the thing those letters mean.

I have strain'd the spider's thread
'Gainst the promise of a maid;
I have weigh'd a grain of sand
'Gainst her plight of heart and hand;
I told my true love of the token,
How her faith proved light, and her
  word was broken:
Again her word and truth she plight,
And I believed them again ere night.

GEORGE GORDON, LORD BYRON (1788–1824)

She Walks in Beauty

She walks in beauty, like the night
Of cloudless climes and starry skies;
And all that's best of dark and bright
Meet in her aspect and her eyes:
Thus mellowed to that tender light
Which heaven to gaudy day denies.

One shade the more, one ray the less,
Had half impaired the nameless grace
Which waves in every raven tress,
Or softly lightens o'er her face;
Where thoughts serenely sweet express
How pure, how dear their dwelling-place.

And on that cheek, and o'er that brow,
So soft, so calm, yet eloquent,
The smiles that win, the tints that glow,
But tell of days in goodness spent,
A mind at peace with all below,
A heart whose love is innocent!

EDWIN MORGAN (b. 1920)

Floating off to Timor

If only we'd been strangers
we'd be floating off to Timor,
we'd be shimmering on the Trades
in a blue jersey boat
with shandies, flying-fish,
a pace of dolphins
to the copra ports.
And it's no use crying
to me, What Dolphins?
for I know where they are
and I'd have snapped you up
and carried you away
if we had been strangers.

But here we are care
of the black roofs.
It's not hard to find
with a collar turned up
and a hoot from the Clyde.
The steps come home
whistling too. And a kettle
steams the cranes out slowly.
It's living with ships
makes a rough springtime
and who is safe
when they sing and blow
their music — they seem
to swing at some light rope
like those desires
we keep for strangers.
God, the yellow deck
breathes, it heaves spray
back like a shout.

We're cutting through
some straits of the world
in our old dark room
with salty wings
in the shriek of the dock wind.
But we're caught — meshed
in the fish-scales, ferries,
mudflats, lifebelts
fading into football cries
and the lamps coming on
to bring us in.

We take in
the dream, a cloth from the line
the trains fling sparks on
in our city. We're better awake.
But you know I'd take
you all the same,
if you were my next stranger.

In Glasgow

In my smoochy corner
take me on a cloud
I'll wrap you round
and lay you down
in smoky tinfoil
rings and records
sheets of whisky
and the moon all right
old pal all right
the moon all night

Mercy for the rainy
tyres and the violet
thunder that bring you
shambling and shy
from chains of Easterhouse
plains of lights
make your delight
in my nest my spell
my arms and my shell
my barn my bell

I've combed your hair
and washed your feet
and made you turn
like a dark eel
in my white bed
till morning lights
a silent cigarette
throw on your shirt
I lie staring yet
forget forget

Spanish Love Poems

JARCHAS (11TH–13TH CENTURIES)

Jarchas are the earliest poems written in Spanish. They were written by Arabic and Hebrew poets in Islamic Spain between 11TH and 13TH centuries. The jarcha is a short refrain, or last stanza of a song, in which a love struck girl speaks to her mother or friends about her passion and sorrow. Her lover *(habib)* is usually referred to as 'friend'. The first European lyric known in a modern Romance language is the jarcha by the Jewish poet Yosef al-Katib (Scriba) c. 1042. By their very nature, these primitive poems are very simple, and it is their simplicity which makes them so beautiful and moving.

So much love

So much love, so much love,
My friend, so much love,
My happy eyes are infirmed
And the pain is so bad.

My Lord Ibrahim

My Lord Ibrahim,
Oh name most sweet,
Come to me
By night.
If not, if thou dost detain,
I shall go to thee.
Tell me where
Thou shalt be.

Yes, Oh my lord

Yes, Oh my lord,
Do not kiss
My red lips,
For I shall turn to saffron.

Little mouth of pearls

Little mouth of pearls,
Sweet as honey true,
Come, kiss me
My love, come to me, do.

If thou desirest me

If thou desirest me as a tasty morsel,
Kiss this my string of pearls,
Little mouth of cherries!

ARCRIPRESTE DE HITA (1283–1350)

Doña Endrina

Ah, what a picture's Doña Endrina walking through
the square!
What a figure, what graceful mien, what swanlike neck
so fair,
Such lustrous hair, little mouth, such colour and poise
most rare.
Arrows of love pierce my heart when her eyes release
their flare.

In this world, Oh sweet desire, I love no-one above you;
Time has sped past, and eternity, though in years but two,
That for your love I pine: I love you more than God 'tis true.
I dare not ask some go-between with you my case pursue.

In great woe I come before you to give my lament rein,
This love and desire pierce so deep, I'm left in throbbing pain,
It will not go, will not leave me, will not release the strain:
The more love retreats, the more I die, this I do not feign.

Love

Love to the slowest subtilty can teach,
And to the dumb give fair and flowing speech,
It makes the coward daring, and the dull
And idle diligent and promptness-full.

It makes youth ever youthful; takes from age
The heavy burden of time's pilgrimage;
Gives beauty to deformity; it seem
To value what is valueless and mean.

Praise of Little Women

In a little precious stone what splendor meets the eyes!
In a little lump of sugar how much of sweetness lies!
So in a little woman love grows and multiplies;
You recollect the proverb says, — 'a word unto the Wise.'

A pepper-corn is very small, but seasons every dinner
More than all other condiments, although 'tis sprinkled thinner;
Just so a little woman is, if Love will let you win her.
There's not a joy in all the world you will not find within her.

And as within the little rose you find the richest dyes,
And in the little grain of gold much price and value lies,
As from a little balsam much odor doth arise,
So in a little woman there's a taste of paradise.

Even as a little ruby its secret worth betrays,
Color and price and virtue, in the clearness of its rays, —
Just so a little woman much excellence displays,
Beauty and grace and love and fidelity always.

The skylark and the nightingale, though small and light of wing
Yet warble sweeter in the grove than all the birds that sing;
And so a little woman, though a very little thing,
Is sweeter far than sugar and flowers that bloom in spring.

The magpie and the golden thrush have many a thrilling note
Each as a gay musician doth strain his little throat,
A merry little songster in his green and yellow coat;
And such a little woman is, when Love doth make her dote.

There's naught can be compared to her, throughout the wide
creation;
She is a paradise on earth, — our greatest consolation, —
So cheerful, gay and happy, so free from all vexation;
In fine, she's better in the proof than in anticipation.

If as her size increases are woman's charms decreased,
The surely it is good to be from all the great released.
Now of two evils choose the less — said a wise man of the East,
By consequence, of woman-kind be sure to choose the least.

MARQUÉS DE SANTILLANA (1398–1458)

Song of Love

Whether you love me,
I cannot declare;
But that I love you,
This is do swear.

No other woman
Could I hold so dear;
Not now, nor ever,
Another revere.
When I beheld you, Oh day
Most blest by love's tender prayer,
With my all I endowed you,
This I do swear.

I'm yours, don't doubt it,
So fear no deceit;
To think otherwise,
Would be false conceit.
Since the day I first me you,
My heart is caught in a snare,
And my wits are your captive,
This I do swear.

I love, will love you
Now and evermore;
Will serve you ever
By love's faithful law.
For I've chosen the finest
From amongst all the most fair,
And as truth is my witness,
This I do swear.

GIL VICENTE (1470?–1536?)

Ode to Maidenhood

They say the marriage knot I should tie,
But I'll take no husband, no, not I.

More, I would rather live at my ease,
In these hills doing just as I please,
Than the hazards of fortune to sieze;
Such chance in wedlock I will defy:
They say the marriage knot I should tie,
But I'll take no husband, no, not I.

Mother, a wife I will never be,
A drudge's life I want not to see,
Nor the gifts with which God endowed me,
Perchance badly used as I comply:
They say the marriage knot I should tie,
But I'll take no husband, no, not I.

There does not, nor will ever exist
Such to catch me in some wedding tryst,
For as I well know and fain insist,
I, fully flowered, alone shall lie:
They say the marriage knot I should tie,
But I'll take no husband, no, not I.

FERNANDO DE ROJAS (1475?–1541)

Venus Dawning

Gracious trees with your leafy shade,
Bow your heads when you see perchance
Those lovely eyes your bower invade,
And hold your jealousy in trance.

Stars whose shaft doth glitter and gleam,
Light that guides as Venus dawning,
Will you not rouse him from his dream,
If he slumbers fast this morning?

Song of Dawn

Chattering parrots, nightingales,
What songs you sing to greet the dawn!
Bring me news of my love's travails,
As I wait silent and forlorn.

The midnight hour has past 'er long
But still no sign of thee.
Tell me if another's blithe song
Keeps him away from me.

CRISTÓBAL DE CASTILLEJO (1490?–1550)

To Love

Give me, Love, kisses without end,
Intertwined as hairs on my head,
A thousand and one kisses send;
Then yet a further thousand shed,
And after
Many thousands, another three.
Now, lest some prying eyes should see,
Let us vain scratch out the score,
And recount backwards, as before.

That noble youth

Oh mother dear, that noble youth
I love such as my life, you know,
Yet to him no hope do I show.

He loves me above self, 'tis true,
Though with disdain I slay his heart,
But hurting him I reap my due,
As hurt to myself I impart.
To see him suffer such, forsooth,
My life in sorrow too does grow,
Yet to him no hope do I show.

'Tis better to forget

With love's most woeful debt,
Whether pain or pleasure,
When weighed by good measure,
'Tis better to forget.

Love is a madness, to be sure,
Whether it be sadness or joy,
And nurtured by memory's ploy,
Only forgetting can inure.
To scratch it with danger's beset,
For while clinging to life's treasure,
When weighed by good measure,
'Tis better to forget.

GARCILASO DE LA VEGA (1503–1536)

Sonnet

Thy face is written in my soul

Lady, thy face is written in my soul,
And whenso'er I wish to chant thy praise,
On that illumined manuscript I gaze,
Thou the sweet scribe art, I but read the scroll.
In this dear study all my days shall roll;
And though this book can ne'er the half receive
Of what in thee is charming, I believe
In that I see not, and thus see the whole
With faith's clear eye; I but received my breath
To love thee, my ill Genius shaped the rest;
'Tis now that soul's mechanic act to love thee,
I love thee, owe thee more than I confessed;
I gained life by thee, cruel though I prove thee;
In thee I live, through thee I bleed to death.

SANTA TERESA DE JESÚS (1515–1582)

I die because I do not die

I live but not within myself,
And in this way awaiting lie:
I die because I do not die.

I live a life not truly mine,
Knowing I die of love's accord,
Because I live for Thee, my Lord;
And as Thou wanted me for Thine,
My heart to Thee I did consign,
Whence it released this aching sigh:
I die because I do not die.

This worldly prison cell divine,
Cell of love within which I live,
Has rendered God as my captive,
And frees my heart which did repine,
And does such passion in me enshrine.
Now God's my prisoner I cry:
I die because I do not die.

How wearisome this earthly life!
How hard to languish in exile!
This prison cell, these chains to vile,
In which this soul endures such strife!
Full yearning to leave my heart's rife
With pain so fierce that I reply:
I die because I do not die.

BALTASAR DEL ALCÁZAR (1530–1606)

Sonnet

Woman's jealousy

Talk not to me of all the frowns of fate,
Or adverse fortune; nor offend my ears
With tales of slavery's suffering in Algiers,
Nor galley's chains, heavy, disconsolate.
Speak not to me of fetter'd maniacs' woes,
Nor proud one from his glory tumbled down:
Dimm'd honour, — friend-abandon'd, — broken crown:
These may be heavy sorrows; but who knows
To bend his head beneath the storms of life
With holy patience, — he the shock will bear,
And see the thundering clouds disperse away.
But give no mortal man a jealous wife, —
Then misery, — galleys, — fetters, — frowns, — dispair, —
loss, — shame, — dishonour, — folly: — What are they?

FERNANDO DE HERRERA (1534–1597)

Sonnet
Pure Spirit

Pure Spirit! that within a form of clay
Once veiled the brightness of thy native sky;
In dreamless slumber sealed thy burning eye,
Nor heavenward sought to wing thy flight away!
He that chastised thee did at length unclose
Thy prison doors, and give thee sweet release,
Unloosed the mortal coil, eternal peace
Received thee to its stillness and repose.
Look down once more from thy celestial dwelling,
Help me to rise and be immortal there —
An earthly vapor melting into air; —
For my whole soul with secret ardor swelling,
From earth's dark mansion struggles to be free,
And longs to soar sway and be at rest with thee.

ANONYMOUS (17TH CENTURY)

Amaryllis

(from *Silva de Romances*)

She sleeps; — Amaryllis
Midst flowerets is laid;
And roses and lilies
Make the sweet shade.

The maiden is sleeping,
Where through the green hills,
Manzanares is creeping
Along with his rills.

Wake not amaryllis,
Ye winds in the glade!
Where roses and lilies
Make the sweet shade.

The sun, while upsoaring,
Yet tarries awhile,
The bright rays adoring
Which stream from her smile.

The wood-music still is
To rouse her afraid,
Where roses and lilies
Make the sweet shade.

LOPE DE VEGA (1562–1635)

Who kills wearing cruelty's glove?

Who kills wearing cruelty's glove?
Love.
On what fare does restlessness feed?
Jealousy's seed.
With what ill is my dearest torn?
Scorn.
What, moreo'er, do such forces spawn,
But a life without hope and joy,
For three things my being destroy,
By name: love, jealousy and scorn.

What result my bold existence?
Persistence.
What end will my suffering meet?
Deceit.
Who fights against my love so dear?
Fear.
Perforce does cruelty appear,
And 'tis but madness to insist,
For the joining one should resist
Of: persistence, deceit and fear.

What emblem does love bid me wear?
Care.
And what is it I most request?
Oblivion's nest.
What does the good I see inspire?
Desire.
Persisting in such madness dire
That my enemy lies within,
Soon these horsemen will do me in:
Care, oblivion and desire.

My woe never brought happiness.
Unhappiness.
On what does my hope want to glance?
Chance.
What counters and thwarts love's essence?
Absence.
For where shall I find the patience,
Though of death I ask it in strife,
If these things end taking my life:
Unhappiness, chance and absence.

FRANCISCO DE QUEVEDO (1580–1645)

Sonnet
Defining Love

It is scorching ice, it is freezing fire,
It is a painful wound that doth not ache,
A sweet dream, but bitterness when awake,
It is a brief repose that doth so tire.

A careless moment that doth care acquire,
It is a coward who brave name doth take,
A lonely walk among the crowd a quake,
A loving just to be loved, nought higher.

It is freedom to a prison cell lured,
That endures unto everlasting life,
An illness that worsens if it's cured.

This is young Cupid, his abyss is a rife.
To all kinds of friendship he is inured,
He whom paradox has riven with strife.

PEDRO CALDERÓN DE LA BARCA (1600–1681)

Love, love

(from El Mágico Prodigioso)

A Voice Within:
What is the glory far above
All else in human life?

All: Love! love!

The First Voice:
There is no form in which the fire
Of love its traces his impressed not.
Man lives far more in love's desire
Than by life's breath, soon possessed not.
If all that lives must love or lie,
All shapes on earth, or sea, or sky,
With one consent, to Heaven cry
That the glory far above
All else in life is —

All: Love! O, love!

Justina: Thou melancholy thought, which art
So fluttering and so sweet, to thee
When did I give the liberty
Thus to afflict my heart?
What is the cause of this new power
Which doth my fevered being move,
Momently raging more and more?
What subtle pain is kindled now,
Which from my heart doth overflow
Into my senses?

All: Love ! O, love!

GUSTAVO ADOLFO BÉCQUER (1836–1870)

Rhyme XI

I am dusky, I am a flame

I am dusky, I am a flame
I am the symbol of passion,
Brimful pleasure my soul doth claim;
Thou seekest me?
— No, not thee.

My brow is pale, my tresses gold,
I offer thee abiding joys,
Of tenderness, I treasures enfold;
Thou callest me?
— No, not thee.

I am a dream, inpalpable,
A vague phantom of mist and light,
Disembodied, I'm intangible;
I cannot love thee.
— O, come! come to me!

Rhyme XVII

Today heaven and earth

Today heaven and earth smile on me,
Today, with the sun's rays my soul is shot,
Today I saw her . . . I saw her and she gave me a glance . . .
Today I believe in God!

Rhyme XXI
What is poetry?

What is poetry?, you say
As you fix my eyes with yours of blue.
What is poetry! . . . You ask me that?
Poetry . . . It is you!

Rhyme XXII
How liveth next to thy heart?

How liveth next to thy heart
That rose so tightly clasped?
A flower next to a volcano till now
I never saw in this world so vast.

Rhyme XXIII
For a glance

For a glance: the world;
For a smile: the heavens;
For a kiss . . . I don't know
What I'd give for a kiss!

Rhyme XXX
A tear swelled up

Within her eye a tear swelled up,
And a word of forgiveness on my lips hung;
Pride then spoke and stifled her sob,
And the word expired on my tongue.

I take one path, she another;
But, thinking on our love once deep,
I still ask: why did I not speak that day?
And she asks: why did I not weep?

Rhyme XXXVIII
Sighs are air

Sighs are air and go to the air.
Tears are water and to the sea flow.
Tell me, woman: knowest thou,
When love's forgot, where it doth go?

ROSALÍA DE CASTRO (1837–1885)

I love you . . . Why do you hate me?

I love you . . . why do you hate me?
— I hate you . . . Why do you love me?
A sad and most mysterious
Secret of the heart is this.

Yet it is true . . . An arduous
And excruciating truth!
— You hate me, because I love you;
I love you, because you hate me.

ANTONIO MACHADO (1875–1939)

The street in shade

The street in shade. The rooftops high of old houses now veil
The dying sun; echoes of light over balconies sail.

Can't you see, midst that charming window with flowers inset,
The rose-coloured oval of a visage remembered yet?

The reflection, in a pane of equivocal image,
Surges and fades like some daguerreotype of old vintage.

In the stillness of the street only your footsteps are heard;
The remaining echoes of twilight slowly become blurred.

Oh anguish! My heavy heart aches . . . Can it perchance be she?
It cannot be . . . Walk on . . . In the blue above, a star I see.

Lord, Thou didst wrench

Lord, Thou didst wrench from me what I most cherished.
Dear God, hear once more my heart's pitiful groan.
Thy will was done, Lord, against what I most wished,
My heart and the sea, Lord, are now left alone.

Ukrainian Love Poems

FOLKSONG

Why Didn't You Come?

Why didn't you come,
When the moon was high?
I was waiting for you.
Did not you have a horse?
Did not you know the way?
Was your Mother against it?

I did have a horse.
I did know the way
And Mother let me go.
My youngest sister,
May she never grow up,
Had hidden my saddle.

But my older sister
Found the saddle
And saddled the horse
-"Go, my dear brother,
To your beloved
Who is waiting for you."

"A little river flows
A very small river,
I will jump over it.
Marry me away,
M dearest Mother
To the one I love."

YOSYP (18TH CENTURY)

Under the Sour Cherry Tree, Under the Sweet Cherry Tree

Under the sour cherry tree, under the sweet cherry tree,
Stood an old man with a young wife, like with a raspberry.
She was asking him, she was begging him:
"— Let me go, old man, out on the street to have some fun!"
"— I will not go there, and I will not let you go there,
All you want is to leave me, because I am an old man.
I will buy you a house, and a hayfield,
And a bench, and a quern, and a cherry tree orchard!"
"— I do not want a house, nor a hayfield,
Nor a bench, nor a quern, nor a cherry tree orchard!
O you, old man, you are all bent like a bow,
But I am young, and I would love to have some fun . . .
O you old bones, may you dry-up and vanish,
But do not dry-up, do not crumble my youth!
You are in the stove (ingle) niche: coughing!
I am with a young man laughing!
O you sleep all the time, and I am crying, and wasting
my years!"

TARAS SHEVCHENKO (1814–1861)

Meditation: Forceful Wind . . .

Forceful wind, forceful wind!
You who speak to the sea, —
Wake it up, play with it,
Question the blue sea.
It knows where my love is,
Because it carried him,
The blue sea will tell you
What it did with him.
If the Sea drowned him —
Then create a storm;
I will go to find my love,
And I will drown my sorrow,
I will drown my misfortune,
And become a mermaid,
I will search the black waves,
and reach the bottom of the sea.
I will find him and take him in my arms
And faint on his chest.
The wave, carry me with my love,
Where the wind blows!
When my love is over the sea,
Dearest wind, you know
Where he walks, what he does
You converse with him.
When he cries — I too cry,
When he does not —I sing;
But if my dark-browed love has perished
Then, I too am dying.
Then carry my soul
Wherever my love is;
Place my soul as a guelder-rose tree
On his grave.
So that the foreign soil of his resting place
Will be lighter to the orphan.

LESIA UKRAINKA (1871–1913)

Mavka's Quest

"Among humans, do couples wed and stay together for a long
time?"
"Of course, forever!"
"Ah! The doves are like that.
Sometimes I observed them and envied them.
They love each other so tenderly and sweetly.
As for me, I do not know anything
Sweeter than the birch tree,
That is why I call it my little sister;
But she is too pale and sad in my opinion;
She is too sad with her head bowed down full of sorrow.
Often she makes me weep, just looking at her.
I do not like the alder (tree) — it is too rough.
The aspen or trembling poplar somehow frightens me;
It seems also afraid of itself — trembling so, all the time.
The oak trees are too serious. Brier, the wild rose,
Is too prickly and so are the hawthorns and the black thorn.
Proud are the ash tree, the maple and the plane-sycamore.
The guelder-rose is so wrapped up in her beauty,
And does not care anymore for anything else in this world.
It seems that I was like her last year.
Now something happened to me and I feel
I am a stranger in my own dear woods.
I feel very much alone! . . ."

Mavka's Bequest

"O do not worry about the body!
It blazed up with a bright flame
Pure, strong, like a good wine.
It became free sparks flying upward.
  Light floating ash, it will, in its turn
Settle down, returning to the native land
Together with water's help, a weeping willow will grow
It will be my end and my beginning!
  People will come
Poor and wealthy, happy and sad,
Bringing me joy and sorrow.
To them, my soul shall speak.
  I shall answer them
With the soft noise of the quivering leaves,
With murmuring willow branches
With the delicate voice of a gentle slender flute
And the sad dew of my branches.
  Then I shall sing to them
Everything: all that once, you sang to me, long ago,
In Uray's Spring; as once you played
Collecting dreams in the forest's groves and depths.
  Play, my Love, play, I do beseech thee!"

PAVLO TYCHYNA (1891–1967)

You Know How the Linden Tree Whispers . . .

You know how the linden tree whispers
In the springtime, at night, by the light of the moon?
  My love sleeps, my love sleeps,
  Let's go and wake her up, kiss her eyes.
  My love sleeps . . .
You heard because of the way the linden tree whispers.

Do you know how the old grove sleeps?
It sees everything, even through the fog.
  Here is the moon, here are the stars, the nightingales . . .
  "I am yours," overheard the old grove.
  And those nightingales . . .
Well! You already know, how the old grove sleeps!

VASYL' GRENDZHA-DONS'KYI (1897–1974)

The Odorant Acacias Were in Bloom

The odorant acacias were in bloom,
And a row of flowering white lilies,
And so were the lilies-of-the-valley,
And the periwinkle was as green as ever,
The little village was thriving in merry walks
And it felt so good here on the fortress,
When I was coming here with her for a promenade,
Escorting her, holding her hand . . .
It is all gone,
But not forgotten!

Of the most beautiful flowers in little gardens,
Only the stems stand out, —
And so it is of our love,
Which, alas, did not end in a wedding! . . .
It felt so good, here, in the springtime,
A warm little wind was blowing,
But then it blew in the cold winter,
And with it, the end for love and pleasures! . . .
It is all gone,
But not forgotten!

MYKOLA HORBAL' (b. 1941)

My Lemko Woman

You write that you are waiting for me
O how good it is to know you are waiting,
When it is so uneasy and uncomfortable,
I wrap myself in your waiting and I am feeling warmer.

My Lemko woman,
    My queen
Do you exist, my love,
    Or maybe not?
Or perhaps indeed you wait for me
    And look for me somewhere.
So why am I so afraid
    That we may not find each other?
Why do I get so frightened
    That we may not meet?
And why does this thought turn my heart to ice,
    My Lemko woman?

Not once did I see
How the girls make wreaths for the feast of Kupala.
And throwing them into the river,
Each one whispers the name of the loved one.

My Lemko woman . . .

Yesterday I dreamt that I was in a meadow
And we, holding hands, were going through the empty city's streets.
I, wearing a torn shirt and bare of foot . . .
I cannot even glance at your face
Because from every window people are looking at us,
And so I did not get to know you.

My Lemko woman . . .

I have such a longing for someone who would write me a
letter . . .

My Lemko woman . . .

ROMAN KUDLYK (b. 1941)

Why Do I Love You?

You ask me
Why do I love you?

. . . Well, when you kiss me
Violins are playing . . .
And is there anything more delicate in the whole world
Than violins?

You ask me
Why do I love you?

. . . Well, when you say:
"Dearest Roman . . . "
I remember my Mother . . .
And is there anyone closer to you in the whole world
Than Mother?

You ask me
Why do I love you?

. . .Well, your hair
Is like a wheat field . . .
And is there something in the whole world
That is more holy than bread?

You ask me
Why do I love you?

. . .Well, your eyes
Are like the waves of the Dnipro River . . .
And is there something, in the whole world,
That is more mine than Ukraine?

You ask me
Why do I love you?

Other Love Poetry from Hippocrene . . .

CLASSIC AMERICAN LOVE POEMS
This anthology contains over 100 inspiring love poems from 47 American poets, encompassing works from colonial days to the twentieth century.
135 pages • 6 x 9 • illus. • $17.50hc • 0-7818-0645-3 • (731)

CLASSIC ENGLISH LOVE POEMS
edited by Emile Capouya
A charmingly illustrated gift edition which includes 95 classic poems of love from English writers.
130 pages • 6 x 9 • illus. • $17.50hc • 0-7818-0572-4 • (671)

CLASSIC FRENCH LOVE POEMS
This volume contains over 25 beautiful illustrations by famous artist Maurice Leloir and 120 inspiring poems translated into English from French, the language of love itself.
130 pages • 6 x 9 • illus. • $17.50hc • 0-7818-0573-2 • (672)

HEBREW LOVE POEMS
edited by David C. Gross
Includes 90 love lyrics from biblical times to modern day, with illustrations by Shagra Weil.
91 pages • 6 x 9 • illus. • $14.95pb • 0-7818-0430-2 • (473)

IRISH LOVE POEMS: DÁNTA GRÁ
edited by Paula Redes
This striking collection includes illustrations by Peadar McDaid and poems that span four centuries up to the most modern of poets, Nuala Ni Dhomhnaill, Brendan Kennelly, and Nobel Prize winner, Seamus Heaney.
146 pages • 6 x 9 • illus. • $17.50hc • 0-7818-0396-9 • (70)

SCOTTISH LOVE POEMS: A PERSONAL ANTHOLOGY
edited by Lady Antonia Fraser
Lady Fraser collects the loves and passions of her fellow Scots, from Burns to Aileen Campbell Nye, into a book that will find a way to touch everyone's heart.
253 pages • 5½ x 8¼ • illus. • $14.95pb • 0-7818-0406-X • (482)

TREASURY OF LOVE PROVERBS FROM MANY LANDS
This anthology includes more than 600 proverbs on love from over 50 languages and cultures.
119 pages • 6 x 9 • illus. • $17.50hc • 0-7818-0563-5 • (698)

TREASURY OF LOVE QUOTATIONS FROM MANY LANDS
This charmingly illustrated, one-of-a-kind gift volume contains over 500 quotations about love from over 50 countries and languages.
120 pages • 6 x 9 • illus. • $17.50hc • 0-7818-0574-0 • (673)

TREASURY OF WEDDING POEMS, QUOTATIONS AND SHORT STORIES
This charming treasury contains over 100 classic poems, quotations and short stories—all on the subject of weddings.
142 pages • 6 x 9 • illus. • $17.50hc • 0-7818-0636-4 • (729)

LONGING FOR A KISS: LOVE POEMS FROM MANY LANDS
This unique anthology contains over 100 love poems from around the world—each one on the all-important subject of the kiss.
196 pages • 6 x 9 • illus. • $19.95hc • 0-7818-0671-2 • (769)

Bilingual Love Poetry from Hippocrene . . .

TREASURY OF LOVE POEMS BY ADAM MICKIEWICZ
in Polish and English
Compiled and edited by Krystyna S. Olszer
137 pages • 5 x 7 • $11.95hc • 0-7818-0652-6 • W • (735)

TREASURY OF AFRICAN LOVE POEMS AND PROVERBS
Nicholas Awde, editor and translator
128 pages • 5 x 7 • $11.95hc • 0-7818-0483-3 • W • (611)

TREASURY OF ARABIC LOVE POEMS, QUOTATIONS AND PROVERBS
Farid Bitar, editor and translator
128 pages • 5 x 7 • $11.95hc • 0-7818-0395-0 • W • (71)

TREASURY OF CZECH LOVE POEMS, QUOTATIONS AND PROVERBS
Marcela Rýdlová-Ehrlich, editor and translator
128 pages • 5 x 7 • $11.95hc • 0-7818-0571-6 • W • (670)

TREASURY OF FINNISH LOVE POEMS, QUOTATIONS AND PROVERBS
Börje Vähämäki, editor and translator
128 pages • 5 x 7 • $11.95hc • 0-7818-0397-7 • W • (118)

TREASURY OF FRENCH LOVE POEMS, QUOTATIONS AND PROVERBS
Richard A. Branyon, editor and translator
128 pages • 5 x 7 • $11.95hc • 0-7818-0307-1 • W • (344)
Audiobook: 0-7818-0359-4 • $12.95 • W • (580)

TREASURY OF GERMAN LOVE POEMS, QUOTATIONS AND PROVERBS
Alumut Hille, editor
109 pages • 5 x 7 • $11.95hc • 0-7818-0296-2 • W • (180)
Audiobook: 0-7818-0360-8 • $12.95 • W • (577)

TREASURY OF HUNGARIAN LOVE POEMS, QUOTATIONS AND PROVERBS
Katherine Gyékenyesi Gatto, editor and translator
128 pages • 5 x 7 • $11.95hc • 0-7818-0477-9 • W • (550)

TREASURY OF INDIAN LOVE: POEMS & PROVERBS FROM THE INDIAN SUB-CONTINENT
Christopher Shackle & Nicholas Awde, editors
128 pages • 5 x 7 • $11.95hc • 0-7818-0670-4 • W • (768)

TREASURY OF IRISH LOVE POEMS, PROVERBS AND TRIADS
Gabriel Rosenstock, editor
153 pages • 5 x 7 • $11.95hc • 0-7818-0644-5 • W • (732)
Audiobook: 0-7818-0748-4 • $12.95 • W • (14)

TREASURY OF ITALIAN LOVE POEMS, QUOTATIONS AND PROVERBS
Richard A. Branyon, editor and translator
128 pages • 5 x 7 • $11.95hc • 0-7818-0352-7 • W • (587)
Audiobook: 0-7818-0366-7 • $12.95 • W • (581)

TREASURY OF JEWISH LOVE POEMS, QUOTATIONS AND PROVERBS,
in Hebrew, Yiddish and Ladino
David Gross, editor
128 pages • 5 x 7 • $11.95hc • 0-7818-0308-X • W • (346)
Audiobook: 0-7818-0363-2 • $12.95 • W • (579)

TREASURY OF POLISH LOVE POEMS, QUOTATIONS AND PROVERBS
Miroslaw Lipinski, editor and translator
125 pages • 5 x 7 • $11.95hc • 0-7818-0297-0 • W • (185)
Audiobook: 0-7818-0361-6 • $12.95 • W • (576)

TREASURY OF ROMAN LOVE POEMS, QUOTATIONS AND PROVERBS
Richard A. Branyon, editor and translator
128 pages • 5 x 7 • $11.95hc • 0-7818-0309-8 • W • (348)

TREASURY OF RUSSIAN LOVE POEMS, QUOTATIONS AND PROVERBS
Victorya Andreyeva, editor
128 pages • 5 x 7 • $11.95hc • 0-7818-0298-9 • W • (591)
Audiobook: 0-7818-0364-0 • $12.95 • W • (586)

TREASURY OF SPANISH LOVE POEMS, QUOTATIONS AND PROVERBS
Juan Serrano and Susan Serrano, editors
128 pages • 5 x 7 • $11.95hc • 0-7818-0358-6 • W • (589)
Audiobook: 0-7818-0365-9 • W • $12.95 • (584)

TREASURY OF UKRAINIAN LOVE POEMS, QUOTATIONS AND PROVERBS
Hélène Turkewicz-Sanko, editor
128 pages • 5 x 7 • $11.95hc • 0-7818-0517-1 • W • (650)

Prices subject to change without notice.
To order Hippocrene Books, contact your local bookstore, call (718) 454-2366, or write to: **Hippocrene Books**, 171 Madison Ave. New York, NY 10016. Please enclose check or money order adding $5.00 shipping (UPS) for the first book and $.50 for each additional title.